The World of My Little Pony®

The Unauthorized Guide to Pony Collectibles

Debra L. Birge
Illustrated by Ann Stroth

4880 Lower Valley Road, Atglen, PA 19310 USA

Dedication

I dedicate this book to pony lovers everywhere.

About The Illustrator

This book was illustrated by Ann Stroth, a freelance photographer in Lexington, Kentucky. She has done many pamphlets and materials for collectors of all sorts. She does beautiful work, thank you Ann.

Designed by "Sue"
Type set in Humanist 521 BT heading font/text font Impress BT

ISBN: 0-7643-1013-5
Printed in China
1 2 3 4

Published by Schiffer Publishing Ltd.
4880 Lower Valley Road
Atglen, PA 19310
Phone: (610) 593-1777; Fax: (610) 593-2002
Please visit out web site catalog at
www.schifferbooks.com or write for a free catalog.
This book may be purchased from the publisher.
Please include $3.95 for shipping.

In Europe, Schiffer books are distributed by
Bushwood Books
6 Marksbury Ave.
Kew Gardens
Surrey TW9 4JF England
Phone: 44 (0)208 392-8585; Fax: 44 (0)208 392-9876
E-mail: Bushwd@aol.com
Free postage in the UK and Europe; air mail at cost

Please try your bookstore first.

We are interested in hearing from authors
with book ideas on related subjects.

Contents

Acknowledgments

I would like to recognize a few people, who have helped me to make this book a great success. Thank you everyone. You all are great!

I would like to thank my dad, Wesley Birge, who bought me numerous ponies when I was young, and my mom, Barbara Birge, who has taken me to countless flea markets over the years in my search for ponies. I would also like to thank Philip Hopper, who has been a great friend to my mother and me, and who helped get this book into print.

The following people have graciously loaned or donated their ponies, pony items, or pictures of their ponies for my book.

Linda (GramaDoll) Waite loaned mail order sparkle pony, Star Hopper, for photos.

Stephanie Stair donated the ponies, Chrysanthemum, mail order pony Twinkler, Hollywood, Baby Hushabye, Baby Rattles, Baby Cha Cha, and Baby Crumpet's Purse for photos.

Beckie Basset donated Baby Blue Ribbon's board game, and a photo of So Soft Satin Lace.

Julie Brix donated a picture of the Mylar wall decorations.

Betsy Groff gave me some pony Shrinky Dinks and Paintable Pony Statues.

My Little Pony® and associated products are registered trademarks of Hasbro., Inc. Hasbro, Inc., did not authorize this book nor furnish or approve of any of the information contained therein. This book is derived from the author's independent research.

Pony Poems

Debra Birge

A Pony Friend

Up in the sky
Down on the earth
Dancing and prancing they
Come to say hi
They swim with the fish
Or stay by your side
When you get down
They are always around
Cheering you up inside
With their happiness
They are always happy to lend
What more could you ask for
Than a little pony friend!

Sweet and Dear from Toe to Ear

They come prancing
and they come a dancing.
They come furry
and get loved in a hurry.
They come sparkly eyed
or with designs on their side.
They come with fancy diapers
and race cars with out drivers.
They come with birds
or pretty bouquets of flowers
They come with snowflakes
and even with a delicious cake
But above all they all come to hold
a special place in our hearts.

Introduction

I have been asked by many people to identify and name ponies for them. I love to help out, but it gets a little overwhelming after a while. Now you can identify your own ponies! I have made available everything that I know and love about ponies in this book. It gives a detailed description of each pony and any additional information about them. There are some variations in hair and body color, and possibly designs, and I have noted these where applicable. This book will allow you and your friends to figure out what ponies you have, and the names of your most wanted ones. Hopefully, many of your questions will be answered with this book. I do not know about every pony that exists, but what I do know is now available here for you to use and learn. My information for this book came from various types of items that I saved (backs of packages, order forms, checklists, and more) throughout the years of my collecting.

This is my third book about My Little Ponies®, and I hope to have more as I discover new and exciting information. This book has been organized in an easy to use manner. It has a table of contents and an index of pony names. The types and descriptions are conveniently located next to the picture of the ponies. The first section helps you to distinguish a real My Little Pony. There are many items that are made to resemble My Little Pony products and these are called "knock-offs." The next section in my book will help you identify your pony and determine whether or your pony is a baby or an adult and what type your pony could possibly be. The third section is a defined list of terms that are used in my book and in the pony world. The ponies are divided in to three sections: Adults, Babies, and Adult & Baby Sets. After the ponies come the Animal Families, which consist of one mommy and two babies. They are followed by the Gift Packs & Sets, Pony Places & Accessories, Pony Clothes, and items that contain pony logos. The Came With section, is where I have listed the accessory items that came with the ponies in their original package.

A True My Little Pony

Not everyone knows the difference between a My Little Pony item and a non-My Little Pony item. My Little Ponies are made from a vinyl/rubber material, and all have silky manes and tails. They were made by Hasbro, and came in many different types and varieties between 1981 and 1991. They have designs on their rump and sometimes all over their sides. A true My little Pony will always have a date and "Hasbro" stamped in one foot. The date is the year the pony's pose was first introduced, not the year the pony was made. Other markings are "pat. pend." in a foot and where they were made in another foot, (e.g., Hong Kong, China, or Thailand). The ponies below are new ones re-released by Hasbro in 1997 and are not included in this book. My book is only about the American ponies made from 1981-1991.

New My Little Ponies made from 1997-1999. These are not included in this book.

Below are various markings found in pony feet. The photo below shows the difference between the "Show Stable" Lemon Drop, which only had markings in two feet, and "Playset" Lemon Drop, which had markings in all four feet.

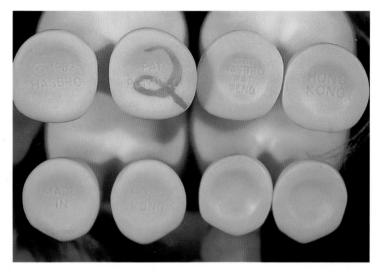

Playset Lemon Drop's feet and Show Stable Lemon Drop's feet

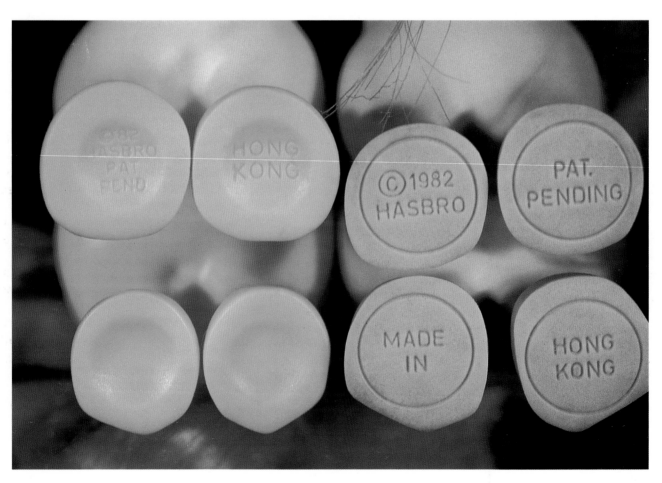

Other common markings found on ponies' feet.

Is It A My Little Pony?

Pictured and described below are a bunch of ponies and animals that are most often times assumed to be or to go with My Little Ponies (MLPs), but really do not.

Left to right: Knock-off of Drink-N-Wet, Hairy Hasbro Dog(Sweetie Pup), Remco pony, Fairy Tail Bird, Snail Key Keeper, Hairy Hasbro Cat, Hasbro Cat, Hairy Hasbro Dog(Sweetie Pup), Remco pony, Remco pony, Hasbro Cat, and Hairy Hasbro Cat. At the lower right are three small knock-offs.

1) Hasbro Fairy Tale birds are not My Little Pony related. These are birds that have really long flowing tails with feet that clip onto things. They are very beautiful, but not My Little Pony. I was told they were in a mail order pamphlet with My Little Ponies. This is why they are assumed to go with My Little Ponies, but they are not pony friends.

2) Hasbro Dogs & Cats have long, and very poofy hair all over them. They were made by Hasbro, but were a totally separate series from MLPs.

3) Hasbro Cats. There were some cats made by Hasbro. They have a long hair tail and forelock. When you pull the tail their forelock gets shorter and if you pull the forelock their tail shortens. Again, these were a separate series and are not My Little Pony Friends!

4) Remco ponies will have Remco written on it somewhere.

They usually have painted hooves and an undetailed design, if any at all.

5) Cabbage Patch Ponies. I think they were made by Hasbro, but I am not sure. They look very bloated with a big head, usually stiff hair, and weird designs.

6) Soma animals will say Soma on it somewhere. They usually have multi-colored, stiff, false hair, and undetailed designs.

7) Horse. They kind of resemble a horse with funky molded feet, and have hair all the way from their nose to their back; really funny looking!

If it does not look like anything pictured in my book then you can be pretty sure it is not a My Little Pony or related item!

Adult or Baby?

Most of the time it is easy to distinguish between a baby or an adult, one is smaller than the other. There are, however, some ponies that are small, but are not babies. These are the adult ponies most commonly assumed to be babies:

A) A small pony with flexible wings that is either a "Windy Winged" or a "Summer Winged Pony." They stand about 3 3/4 inches tall.

B) "Flutter Ponies," which are 4 inches tall with long legs and have a clip on their back to hold their wings. Their wings are so fragile they usually are found without them. Sometimes even the clip is gone and a hole is left in their back.

C) "Pretty Mane Ponies" are two short ponies with colorful hair and scribbles on their rump. They stand about 3 3/4 inches tall.

Determining the Type of your Pony

All land dwelling ponies can be classified into three groups: pegasus, unicorn, or earthling. A pegasus is a winged pony; wings give them flying ability. A unicorn has a horn, which gives it the ability to wink (disappear and reappear in another location). An earthling is an earth-bound pony with no wings or horn. They possess the magic to spread cheer and happiness whereever they go.

There are also sea dwelling ponies called "Sea Ponies." They are adapted for the water with curled tails and fins. Baby Sea Ponies come with a float ring since they haven't mastered swimming yet. Sea Ponies will be listed after babies in this section. However, they are combined under adults & babies in the main portion of my book.

Adults

Look at your adult, and ask yourself if it has any special features (e.g., gem eyes, flocked body, gem type design, rainbow hair, design all over, long slender legs, wings, weird clip or hole, flat feet, etc.). Most often the pony's features has to do with its type. I have listed special features and what type they could be. If you still have trouble, look through the "List of Terms."

A) A fuzzy pony – "So Soft"
B) Gem eyes – "Twinkle Eyed"
C) Gem designs – "Princess Ponies"
D) Design all over body – "Twice As Fancy," "Sunshine Pony," or "Loving Family Pony"

E) Tall, flower earring – "Sweetheart Sister"
F) Tall, flower earring & glitter designs – "Glitter Sweetheart Sister"
G) Tall, heart-shaped design – "Pretty Pony"
H) Short, long legs, clip holder for wings – "Flutter Ponies"
I) Short, long legs, colorful mane – "Pretty Mane Ponies"
J) Flat feet – "Original Ponies"
K) Rainbow hair, glitter design – "Rainbow Ponies"
L) Rainbow hair curled in locks – "Rainbow Curl Ponies"
M) 3-D design like pocket on one side – "Precious Pocket Ponies"
N) 3-D ice cream designs – "Sundae Best Pony"
O) White/color locks of hair, candy design – "Candy Cane Pony"
P) Berry design, smells – "Sweetberry Pony"
Q) Molded hair around feet – "Big Brother"
R) White body, dark pink mane, flower design – "Birthflower Pony"
S) Long hair, head twists to reel in hair – "Brush 'n Grow"
T) Long hair, head twists to reel in hair, gem on forehead – "Brush 'n Grow Princess Ponies"
U) White, dark pink hair, doll/ball/bear – "Special Pony"
V) Has molded -on decorated saddle, carousel horse – "Merry-Go-Round Pony"
W) Knob on chest – "Dance 'n Prance"
X) Santa or stocking design – "Christmas Ponies"
Y) Hard plastic, looks like horse - Dream Beauty
Z) Glittery see-through bodies – "Sparkle Pony"
AA) See-through bodies with shapes, glows in the dark – "Glow 'n Shows"
BB) Circle around tail, squeeze shoulders and tail twirls – "Happy Tails"
CC) Rub design and picture appears – "Magic Message"
DD) Neon colors, shapes all over – "Rockin Beat Pony"
EE) Puffy hair, smells like perfume – "Perfume Puff"
FF) Goldi locks or rapunzle on rump – "Fairy Tail Pony"
GG) Small with flexible plastic wings – "Windy Wing Pony" or "Summer Wing Pony"
HH) Glittery designs, or nothing special – "Regular Ponies"
II) Jointed, body suit – "Sweetsteps Ballerina"
JJ) Large, hard plastic body, with trigger under chin – "My Pretty Pony"

Babies

Looking at your baby, check for details that stick out right away (e.g., painted on diaper, swiveling head, glittery design, has a tooth, design is all over, moving eyes, kind of small really cute, no design or star). Most often, like the adult, a baby's type has to do with its features as well.

Three very extraordinary babies in a raring pose!
Baby Yo-Yo, pegasus, purple body, pink hair, yo-yo - Original Newborn
Speckles, pink body, yellow hair, pink & blue safety pins - Newborn Twin
Bunkie, yellow body, purple hair, pink & blue safety pins - Newborn Twin

A) Painted-on diaper – "Fancy Pants"

B) Moving eye lids – "Beddy-Bye-Eyed"

C) Swiveling head – "Peek-a-boo Baby"

D) Swiveling head, molded hair around feet – "Peek-a-boo Baby" or "Playtime Baby Brother"

E) Has a tooth – "First Tooth"

F) Design all over body – "Twice As Fancy Baby" or "Loving Family Pony"

G) Pearly finish – "Pearlized Baby"

H) A very small baby, 2-1/2 inches tall – "Teeny Tiny"

I) Glittery designs – "Regular Baby"

J) Jointed, body suit – "Ballerina Baby"

K) Yarn, bees, pockets, clover designs – "Baby Pony & Pretty Pal"

L) No Design or White Star - Baby Ember

M) Horse shoe, sailboat, larger bodied, 3 1/2 inches tall – "Baby Boys"

N) Cupcake or cake design – "Baby Sisters"

O) Balloon dogs – "Party Babies"

P) Chuck E Cheese design – "Chuck E Cheese Baby"

Q) Green stocking – "Kellogg's Baby"

R) Rainbow hair & designs – "Rainbow Babies"

S) Glittery, see-through bodies – "Sparkle Baby"

T) Small newborn baby (slightly bigger than a Teeny Tiny) – "Newborn Twins" or "Original Newborns"

U) Large, hard baby with blinking eyes, 9 1/2 inches tall – "Soft Sleepy Newborn"

V) Blue baby with blue ribbon – "Special Baby Pony"

W) Red heart/rainbow or pink heart/arrow – "Valentines Day Sisters"

Sea Ponies

Hopefully you can tell the difference between a sea pony and a regular pony. However, if you have never seen one before it can kind of throw you at first. A Sea Pony has a curled tail, and no legs, as they are adapted for the water. Adults are about 6 inches long and came in shells. Babies are 4 1/2 inches long and came with float rings.

A) String hair – "Watercolor Baby Sea Pony"

B) Pearly, glossy finish – "Pretty 'n Pearly Baby Sea Pony"

C) Painted on sea shell necklace – "Sea Sparkle Baby Sea Pony"

D) Mermaid with shimmery tail – "Fancy Mermaid Baby"

List of Terms

Below is a list of terms that are used throughout my book and by collectors. I have written what they mean, or stand for, beside them. This list is conveniently placed at the front for you to use whenever you need to.

Baby Ember: a special baby pony with no design or a single white star. .

Baby Pony and Pretty Pal: baby pony and animal friend set; design is related to animal friend

Baby Sisters: two baby sisters, one with a cake design and the other with a cup cake design.

Ballerina Baby: a baby with jointed legs and head, no design

Beddy-Bye-Eyed Baby (BBE): has eyes that open and close

Big Brothers: adult male ponies, molded plastic feathers (heavy hair) around feet

Boy Babies: two of the first boy babies; have either a horse shoe or a sail boat on them

Brush 'n Grows: twist their head and their tail will get shorter; tail can be pulled back out.

Candy Cane Pony: has two colors of hair together in locks, white and another color, and is candy scented

Collector Ponies: the original six ponies remade with pushed in feet from mail order

Dance 'n Prance: hold tail, twist knob on neck, set pony down and she dances as tail spins

Dream Beauties: look like Barbie horses, not like a pony; Hasbro mark in their leg

Drink 'n Wet Baby: has holes in mouth and under tail; she drinks, then wets in her diaper

Earthling: an earthling doesn't have a horn or wings

Fairy Tale Ponies: I call them this, because they were made after fairy tales, Rupunzel and Goldilocks

Fancy Mermaid Baby: pearly and looks like a mermaid part of the "10th Anniversary" series

Fancy Pants Baby: has painted on white diaper with designs all over it

First Tooth Baby: has a small baby tooth in its mouth

Flutter Pony: long legs, thin shiny plastic wings (breaks easily, may have only clip on back)

Glitter Sister: tall with glittery designs all over and a flower earring or a hole if there isn't one.

Glow 'n Show: has shapes in see-through plastic that glow in the dark

Happy Tails: Press their shoulders and their tail will twirl

Loving Family Ponies: look like "Twice as Fancy," but baby has mom's and dad's designs

Magic Message: rub the symbol and an image will appear

Merry-Go-Round: decorated to look like a carousel horse with a colorful saddle as their design.

MLP: Stands for "My Little Pony"

MLPs: Stands for "My Little Ponies"

Newborn Twin Babies: two babies that came together with a toy; most have the same design

Original Ponies: a set of six ponies made with flat feet, not the usual pushed in feet.

Paradise Baby: a really bright neon orange, pink, or yellow baby made for the "10th Anniversary" series

Pearlized Baby: has a pearly gloss finish

Peek-A-Boo Babies: A set of six, 4 girls & 2 boys, that have heads that swivel

Pegasus: a winged pony

Perfume Puff Pony: have really fluffy hair and smell like perfume

Petite Pony: 1 1/4 inches tall, all plastic/molded mane & tail, on a base w/a horseshoe imprint

Playtime Baby Brother: A set of six boys with swiveling heads

Precious Pocket Pony: design makes pocket for an attached related item to fit in. For example, "Bubble Fish" has a fish bowl pocket that holds a fish on an attached string (so you don't loose the fish!!)

Pretty Mane Ponies: 2 short ponies with two colors in their mane (top half one color, bottom half another color) and scribbles as designs.

Pretty-n-Pearly Sea Baby: shimmery colored Sea Baby

Pretty Ponies: tall with slender legs and designs in the shapes of hearts.

Princess Baby: white with glittery castle design and star on forehead - "Princess and Baby Buggy"

Princess Pony: has a 3-D gem design on their hindquarters and tinsel in their hair

Rainbow Baby: has rainbow related design and tri-colored hair

Rainbow Curl Pony: multicolored curled hair in separate curls, some type of rainbow design.

Rainbow Ponies: have four sections of rainbow colored hair. They also have glittery designs.

Regular Sea Baby: does not have any special features

Sea Pony: have curled tails (no legs/feet) the adults are a little over 5 1/2 inches long

Sea Sparkle Sea Baby: has a painted-on shell necklace

Secret Surprise: big pony, back opens up; you can hide treasures in it

So Softs(SS): have fuzz or fur covered body and feel soft to the touch.

Sparkle Pony: adults and babies that have glittery see-through bodies

Summer Winged: small ponies with plastic wings with different colors and designs. They are about 1 3/4" tall with things that fly as designs (e.g., bee, dove, lady bug, etc.)

Sundae Best: a pony with a 3-D ice cream design; is scented.

Sundance Pony: made several different ways, for different sets; see "Sundance Sets."

Sun Shine Pony: has a white/light pink streak in mane and tail that turns dark pink in sun

Sweetberry Ponies: will have some type of berry design (e.g., cranberry muffins, raspberry jam) and is scented

Sweet Heart Sister: tall with slender legs, have a flower bouquet design and wear a flower earring.

Sweet Steps Ballerina: has molded-on workout suit/ballerina shoes, moveable legs; adults have designs; their body color is the color of their legs and head*

10th Anniversary Ponies: last My Little Ponies made by Hasbro, celebrated the 10th anniversary (1991) of pony making!!

Teeny Tiny Baby: smaller than regular baby, tiny in comparison, also check 10th Anniversary "Teeny Pony Twins"

Tropical Pony: tropical colored hair and body, tropical designs

Twice As Fancy (TAF): Adults and babies that have their design up their sides and on cheek or forehead

Twinkle-Eye Pony (TE): has sparkly gem eyes.

Unicorn - a pony with a horn

Valentines Day Twins: a set of two, one is white with a red heart/rainbow over it, the other is purple with a heart/arrow through it.

Water Color Baby Sea Pony: hair and body turns color in warm water, have thread like hair

Wedding Pony: two different "Sweetheart Sister" wedding ponies were made. They are white with white tinsel hair; see also 10th Anniversary

Wedding Couple: a 3rd type of wedding pony that is not a Sweetheart Sister. Look under "Wedding Couple" for information on her and who she came with.

Windy Winged: resemble "Summer Wings," designs are varied, no pattern

There were a variety of adult ponies produced. This section will cover all the American adult ponies. All pictures read left to right and front row to back row. All adults are valued at these conditions:

Mint Condition (M) no hair trims or permanent marks

Great Condition (GR) a couple minor unnoticeable marks, tiny hair snip

Good Condition (G) permanent marks, hair trims, not too bad

Poor (P) really bad off, many marks, hair cut.

Big Brother Ponies

These guys came with a hat and scarf and were produced in two different groups. Their feet have been molded to make them look like they have hair around them.

Big Brothers - Group 1. M=$15, GR=$12, G=$10, P=$5

Salty, green body, purple hair with pink stripe in mane, pink boat: sailor's hat

Quarterback, dark blue body, blue hair white stripe in mane, pink/white football: lavender/pink helmet

Steamer, pink body, pink hair green stripe in mane, yellow/blue train: rail road hat

4-Speed, light blue body, blue hair light pink stripe in mane, pink/purple truck: hard hat

Slugger, purple body, white hair melon stripe in mane, green/white baseball glove with bat: baseball cap

Tex, yellow body, pink hair blue stripe in mane, green cactuses: cowboy hat/ sheriff's badge

Big Brothers - Group 2. M=$15, GR=$12, G=$10, P=$5

Tex, yellow body, pink hair blue stripe in mane, green cactuses: cowboy hat/ sheriff's badge

Chief, white body, blue hair yellow stripe in mane, red hose & yellow ladder: fire hat

Salty, green body, purple hair pink stripe in mane, pink boat: sailor's hat

Barnacle, blue body, red hair gold stripe in mane, red/yellow treasure chest: blue/ white pirates hat

Wigwam, orange body, white hair lt. blue stripe in mane, blue/red teepees: Indian headdress

Steamer, pink body, pink hair green stripe in mane, yellow/blue train: rail road hat

This Big Brother was part of a "wedding couple." Known as Coat 'n Tails when sold when sold separately from Satin 'n Lace in 1988, and Tux 'n Tails when sold with Satin 'n lace as a set in 1990.

Coat 'n Tails or Tux 'n Tails, blue body, blue hair, white bowties, came with blue bowtie

Birthflower Ponies

Available through the mail only, each was named after the flower of its month. All Birthflowers are white with rose pink hair and colored flower designs of their month. M=$20, GR=$15, G=$10, P=$5

Hasbro Birthflower Pony mail order pamphlet

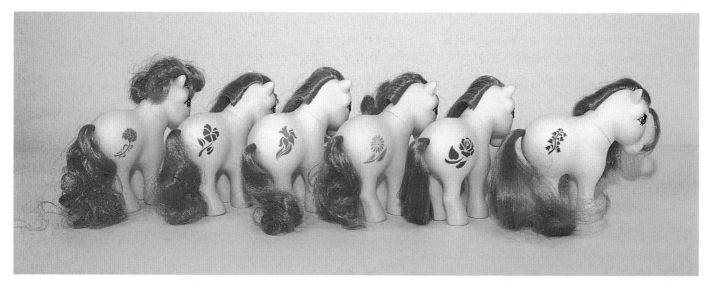

Carnation, white body, rose pink hair, light pink carnation - January
Violet, white body, rose pink hair, purple violet - February
Daffodil, white body, rose pink hair, dark pink daffodil - March
Daisy, white body, rose pink hair, light blue daisy - April
Rose, white body, rose pink hair, red rose - June
Lily of the Valley, white body, rose pink hair, green Larkspur - May

Water Lily, white body, rose pink hair, light blue water lily - July
Poppy, white body, rose pink hair, dark pink poppy - August
Morning Glory, white body, rose pink hair, dark blue morning glory -
  September
Cosmos, white body, rose pink hair, light pink cosmos - October
Chrysanthemum, white body, rose pink hair, orange chrysanthemum
  – November. *Courtesy of Stephanie Stair*
Holly, white body, rose pink hair, green holly - December

Brush 'n Grow Ponies

They have long flowing manes and tails. Their tail can be made shorter by twisting their head, and made long again by turning the head to the pony's right and pulling the tail back out. M=$8, GR=$6, G=$4, P=$2

Ringlets, grayish body, yellow/pink/purple/blue hair, yellow head band
Braided Beauty, pegasus, green body, green/pink/yellow/white hair, pink braided pony tail
Twisty Tail, blue body, red/white/green/yellow hair, yellow brush and comb
Bouquet, unicorn, white body, yellow/pink/blue/red hair, pink hat
Curly Locks, pegasus, purple body, pink/yellow/blue/white hair, blue bow tied on yellow pony tail
Pretty Vision, yellow body, red/green/pink/blue hair, pink mirror

Brush 'n Grow Princess Ponies

They have the same tail feature as the Brush 'n Grows. They also have a colored gem on their forehead, which I have listed at the end of their descriptions. M=$10, GR=$8, G=$6, P=$4

Star Gleamer, blue body, pink/light pink/ yellow hair/pink tinsel, pink & yellow striped stars: pink gem
Skylark, green body, melon/purple hair/ purple tinsel, pink & purple striped birds: purple gem
Glittering Gem, pegasus, pink body, yellow/white/pink hair/multi tinsel, red/yellow hearts: pink gem
Brilliant Bloom, pegasus, purple body, light purple/blue hair/purple tinsel, blue/pink flowers: blue gem

Candy Cane Ponies

They are candy scented with curled locks of hair consisting of white and another color. M=$6, GR=$5, G=$4, P=$1

Molasses, pink body, light blue & white hair, white/blue gingerbread men
Sugar Apple, pegasus, light blue body, pink & white hair, pink & yellow candied apples
Mint Dreams, green body, purple & white hair, purple/white lollipops
Caramel Crunch, purple body, red & white hair, blue/yellow box of popcorn
Sugar Sweet, unicorn, light pink body, light blue/white hair, green/yellow cotton candy on cone
Lemon Treats, yellow body, white & green hair, pink & white slices of cake

Christmas Ponies

Merry Treat was available in stores. Stockings was a special mail order pony only available to My Little Pony Fan Club members. Stockings is a harder to find pony and Merry Treats is moderately hard to find.

Merry Treat, white body, red and green hair, Santa Claus. M=$10, GR=$8, G=$6, P=$4
Stockings, white body, light pink hair, green and pink stocking. M=$20, GR=$15, G=$10, P=$5

Collector's Ponies

These gals were given pushed-in feet for this mail-order set. When they first came out as "Original" ponies in stores the bottoms of their feet were flat. They are fairly common ponies. M=$6, GR=$5, G=$4, P=$1

Snuzzle, light gray body, pink hair, pink hearts
Butterscotch, gold body, gold hair, gold butterflies
Blue Belle, powder blue body, lavender hair, blue stars
Blossom, purple body, purple hair, white blossoms
Minty, mint green body, white hair, green shamrocks
Cotton Candy, pink body, pink hair, white spots

Dance 'n Prance Pony

Each came with earrings and a fuzzy boa. They are wound up by holding their tail and winding the flower on their chest. When they are set down, and their tail is released, they will dance for you. M=$8, GR=$6, G=$4, P=$2

Player, green body, pink hair, white guitar
Songster, orange body, blue hair, green microphone
D.J., unicorn, blue body, yellow hair, yellow boom box
Swinger, yellow body, green hair, pink headphones and music notes
Twirler, unicorn, pink body, pink hair, blue records
Tap Dancer, purple body, pink hair, yellow top hat and cane

Dream Beauties

Hasbro made My Little Pony Dream Beauties. These do not look like usual Little Ponies. They look more like "Barbie" horses. They are about 7 1/2 inches tall to the ear, and most say Hasbro inside a back leg. Body colors are pearly like, and there were six different types made. Dream Beauties are not as easily found as other ponies. All of them are fairly rare.

Highflying Beauty: All have big and plastic wings. M=$25, GR=$20, G=$15, P=$5
> Glider, purple/green wings, white body, pink hair, pegasus design
> *Not shown:* Sky Flier, blue/white wings, purple body blue nose and legs, pink hair, pink & white hearts
> *Not shown:* Wind Walker, ?? wings, blue body, ?? hair, ?? design

Rainbow Beauties: Have rainbow splashes across body. M=$25, GR=$20, G=$15, P=$5
> Wind Sweeper, blue body, white/pink/green/ blue hair, pink/white/blue flower swirls up along sides
> *Not shown:* Sky Splasher, white body, rainbow hair, bird swirl
> *Not shown:* Morning Glory, yellow body, rainbow hair, sun swirl

20

Shimmering Beauty: Resembles a Sparkle Pony. M=$25, GR=$20, G=$15, P=$5
>Crystalline, blue body, white hair, two pink/blue swans
>*Not shown:* Dreamgleamer, dark pink body, pink hair, heart with wings
>*Not shown:* Stardazzle, orange body, dark pink hair, flowered heart

Showtime Beauty: Looks like a carousel horse. M=$25, GR=$20, G=$15, P=$5
>May Fair, pink body, blue hair, purple/white/blue saddle & rose design
>Circle Dancer, purple body, blue hair, shell & bow design

Sweet Perfume Beauty: Medallions on rump open up to reveal perfume for you to wear. M=$25, GR=$20, G=$15, P=$5

Colorglow, purple body with green legs, green/white hair, red heart medallion

Song Rider, blue body with pink legs, pink and white hair, pink star medallion

Fair Flier, pink body with yellow legs, purple/green hair, green bird medallion

Not shown: Color Mist, blue body with light purple legs, white hair/purple stripe in mane, gold flower medallion.

Trim 'n Grow Beauty: They all came with extra hair refills and scissors. M=$25, GR=$20, G=$15, P=$5

Sheertrimmer, gray body, purple mane and pink tail and forelock, pink/purple ring, necklace & earrings

Not shown: Mane Waves, pink body, white tail and forelock and blue mane , yellow vanity

Not shown: Spritzy, purple body, pink/aqua/purple hair, bathtub

Fairy Tale Ponies

Available through mail order only. Each has beautiful curled locks of hair. Rapunzel is a rare pony and can be hard to find. Goldilocks is moderately hard to find.

Rapunzel, pink body, yellow hair/gold streamers, castle & Rapunzel and her long hair hanging down. M=$25, GR=$20, G=$15, P=$5

Goldilocks, pink body, yellow hair, baby bear with porridge. M=$15, GR=$10, G=$5 P=$2

Firefly With Video

Firefly, pegasus, pink body, blue hair, painted on blue lightning bolts. She came with a video called *Firefly's Adventure*. However this Firefly is in a totally different pose than the original Firefly. This Firefly is standing with one leg bent, she is in Heart-Throb's pose. Her colors are the same, but they are darker, the design is the same but is painted on and not glittery! M (w/video)=$30, G=$20, P=$10, M(pony value)=$25, Great=$20, G=$15, Poor=$5.

Flutter Ponies

The wings, If they still have them, are thin and look metallic. Flutter ponies are extremely hard to find with their wings. Their wings are very, very fragile and break extremely easily.

Flutter Ponies - Group 1. No wings: M=$5, GR=$4, G=$3, P=$1; with wings add $20
   Rosedust, yellow body, pink hair, red roses
   Lily, light pink body, lavender hair, green bush with red flowers
   Honeysuckle, light pink body, pink hair, pink/yellow snowflake flower
   Morning Glory, green body, neon yellow hair, green vine with purple flowers
   Forget-Me-Not, purple body, white hair, purple flowers
   Peach Blossom, light blue body, blue hair, pink blossoms

Flutter Ponies - Group 2. No wings: M=$5, GR=$4, G=$3, P=$1; with wings add $20
   Rosedust, yellow body, pink hair, red roses
   Lily, light purple body, lavender hair, green bush with red flowers
   Wind Drifter, yellow body, green hair, red & blue wind mill
   Cloud Puff, purple body, teal hair, white cloud blue wind
   Wingsong, pink body, blue hair, purple music notes
   Tropical Breeze, blue body, red hair, pink flamingo

Other Flutter Ponies produced:
Yum Yum, purple body, green hair, pink candies. Came with "Party Pack"
Hollywood, pink body, white hair, glittery stars. M=$15, GR=$12, G=$10, P=$5; add $10 w/wings. Flutter Pony Hollywood was made for the movie "Hollywood." She was a mail order exclusive. *Courtesy of Stephanie Stair*
Pink Dreams, blue body, pink hair, pink cat. Came with "Slumber Party Pack"

Glitter Sweetheart Sister Ponies

Each are wearing a flower earring. I have listed the color of their earrings at the end of the description. M=$8, GR=$6, G=$5, P=$3

Twinkler, yellow body, gold hair, glittery gold flowers all over, pink flower earring
Sunblossom, pink body, pink hair, glittery silver stars all over, purple flower earring
Starflash, blue body, purple hair, glittery pink hearts all over, pink flower earring
Bright Night, purple body, pink hair, glittery purple bows all over, blue flower earring

Glow 'N Show Ponies

These gals have see-through bodies with shapes in the plastic. These shapes are what glow in the dark! M=$6, GR=$5, G=$4, P=$1

Dazzle Glow, unicorn, purple body, pink/blue hair, yellow umbrellas
Bright Glow, orange body, pink/purple hair, white doves
Star Glow, pegasus, blue body, pink/yellow hair, orange piano and candlestick
Happy Glow, pink body, blue/white hair, blue clown hats

Happy Tails Ponies

Their tails twirl when you squeeze their shoulders. M=$6, GR=$5, G=$4, P=$1

Tossels, pink body, blue hair, white teddy bears

Tall Tales, pegasus, yellow body, blue hair, pink giraffes

Romper, purple body, pink hair, yellow rabbits

Woosie, green body, yellow hair, yellow mice

Tabby, unicorn, pink body, pink hair, blue kittens

Squeezer, blue body, pink hair, yellow bunnies

Hasbro Softies

Hasbro made stuffed ponies called "Hasbro Softies." The stuffed ponies resemble the pony they are made after. The design is sewn on and they stand straight-legged. I know the following stuffed ponies were made: Cotton Candy, Bow Tie, Parasol, Firefly, Blossom, Glory, Windy, Posey, Cherries Jubilee, Moondancer, Star Shine, Mother & Baby sets (1986): Lickity-Split, Surprise, and Lofty. Stuffed babies are extremely hard to find. Adults: M=$10, GR=$8, G=$6, P=$2, Babies: M=$35, GR=$30, G=$20, P=$10. With tags attached add $5 to value.

Applause also made stuffed ponies. I have one and she came with a brush around her neck, and looks exactly like the pony she was made after. Her design is painted on her fur, and she is also in the pose of the pony she was made after. Colors are exact on everything, except that the design color is off a bit. M=$6, GR=$5, G=$4, P=$1

Softie Earthlings, Lickity-Split and Parasol

Softie Pegasi, Mommy and Baby Surprise

Softie Unicorns, Windy and Moondancer

Magic Message Ponies

Most of the time the top layer (a thin colored film) of their design is missing. This part is essential and a big part of the pony's name. You gently rub the top layer to reveal the magic message underneath it. M=$6, GR=$5, G=$4, P=$1

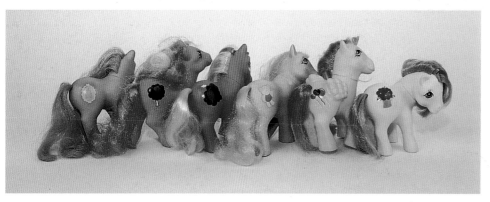

Mirror Mirror, light green body, green hair light pink stripe in mane, gold mirror

Windy, pink body, melon hair yellow stripe in mane, apple tree

Cloud Dreamer, unicorn, pink body, white hair green stripe in mane, cloud

Cuddles, light blue body, yellow hair light pink streak in mane, yellow teddy bear

Floater, pegasus, yellow body, pink hair green stripe in mane, three balloons

Magic Hat, white body, purple hair red stripe in mane, purple rabbit in a hat and wand

McDonald's Ponies

They look like a paper clip at the top and have a charm size pony attached to it. They are about 7 cm tall and 2 1/2 cm wide; the pony itself is 3 cm wide. M=$45, GR=$30, G=$20, P=$10

Minty, mint green body, white hair, green shamrock

Blossom, purple body, purple hair, white blossom

Butterscotch, gold body, gold hair, gold butterfly

Not shown: Snuzzle, light gray body, pink hair, pink heart

Not shown: Blue Belle, powder blue body, lavender hair, blue star

Not shown: Cotton Candy, pink body, pink hair, white specks

Merry-Go-Round Ponies

They are designed like carousel horses! M=$6, GR=$5, G=$4, P=$1

Flower Bouquet, white body, pink hair, yellow saddle area trimmed with white flowers

Sparkler, purple body, blue hair, pink saddle area with blue dots, white tassels

Tassels, light green body, pink hair, purple saddle area with white flowers, pink trim purple lace

Diamond Dreams, yellow body, red hair, purple & pink saddle area with white dots, pink tassels

Sunny Bunch, light purple body, green hair, white saddle area with pink dots, blue/pink flowers. This pony was also remade as a part of the "Scrub-A-Dub Tub" set. No changes can be seen between the two.

Brilliant Blossom, blue body, yellow hair, pink saddle area, white dots/flowers, pink trim

Mummy Charms

They are about the size of Petite Ponies and came with ponies in specially marked packages. They are completely hard plastic with a hole to hang them on a bracelet that was available through the mail. Each have a flower in their mouth. Pony charms help the pony moms remember all the important things that make them really good. M=$10, GR=$8, G=$6, P=$4

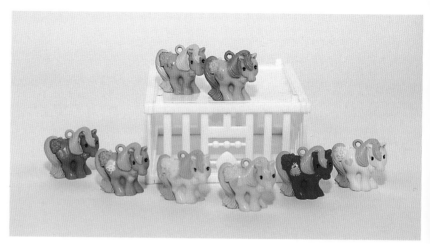

Tell-A-Tale, purple body, pink hair, white book
Paint-A-Picture, blue body, yellow hair, painter's palette
Laugh-A-Lot, yellow body, pink hair, question marks
Fair Play, yellow body, blue hair, megaphone
Little Helper, red body, orange hair, white apron
True Blue, white body blue hair, blue heart
Hugs and Kisses, pink body, light blue hair, Xs & Os
Sweet Tune, blue body, purple hair, orange tuba
Not shown: Ticklish, light pink body, white hair, red feather
Not shown: Fun Lover, white body, light purple hair, party hat
Not shown: Morning Sunshine, light blue body, orange hair, sun
Not shown: Yours Too, yellow body, neon green hair, milk shake
Not shown: Happy Dancer, blue body, orange hair, black tap shoes
Not shown: Tiny Tumbler, orange body, blue hair, trampoline
Not shown: Pretty Please, purple body, blue hair, sugar bowl
Not shown: Sweet and Special, white body, pink hair, pink flowers
Not shown: Sweetheart, pink body, red hair, red heart with arrow through it
Not shown: Secret Keeper, white body, yellow hair, key
Not shown: Funny Face, purple body, yellow hair, smiley face with hat
Not shown: Curtain Call, yellow body, white hair, two masks

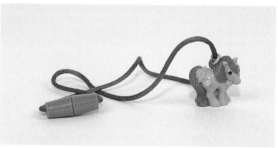

A Sweet Scoops Mummy Charm on a necklace, came with mail order "Sweet Scoops & Pendant" set
Sweet Scoops, purple body, purple hair, purple & white ice cream cone

My Pretty Pony

These were the first ponies produced by Hasbro in 1981. I have found a couple of these big ponies. They stand about 10 inches tall and have a trigger under their chin. When you pull the trigger one eye winks, their ears twitch, and their tail swishes. I have no idea of how many these were made, but I am thinking one for each of the original six designs. Each came with a red saddle and cowboy hat. Often the back seam is splitting; watch this when pricing them. M=$25, GR=$20, G=$10, P=$5

Butterscotch My Pretty Pony

Yellow Peachy My Pretty Pony

Pink Peachy My Pretty Pony

Original Ponies

These are the first original vinyl ponies. The were sold in stores before being made into the Collector's Ponies. These have flat feet, not the convex feet like the other ponies. These gals are fairly common. M=$6, GR=$5, G=$4, P=$1

Cotton Candy, pink body, pink hair, white spots
Minty, mint green body, white hair, green shamrocks
Blossom, purple body, purple hair, white blossoms
Blue Belle, powder blue body, lavender hair, blue stars
Butterscotch, gold body, gold hair, gold butterflies
Snuzzle, light gray body, pink hair, pink hearts

Perfume Puff Ponies

They smell like perfume and have very poofy hair. M=$6, GR=$5, G=$4, P=$1

Sweet Lily, pink body, white hair, blue heart with pink fringe
Sweet Suds, pink body, blue hair, blue bathtub
Dainty Dahlia, gray body, pink hair, yellow perfume sprayer, pink flowers
Daisy Sweet, green body, yellow hair, white perfume sprayer/pink heart
Lavender Lace, pegasus, purple body, green hair, blue perfume sprayer/pink hearts
Red Roses, unicorn, yellow body, pink hair, green perfume sprayer/pink flower

Precious Pocket Ponies

Their design makes a pocket to hold a related item attached by a string. Consider poor condition if pocket is missing. M=$15, GR=$10, G=$5, P=$3

Bunny Hop, white body, pink/purple mane pink tail, purple hat pink bunny
Sweet Pocket, purple body, light pink/blue mane pink tail, pink flower yellow bee
Bubblefish, pink body, pink/blue mane blue tail, fishbowl on pink stand yellow fish
Li'l Pocket, blue body, melon/blue mane blue tail, pink piggy bank yellow coin

Pretty Mane Ponies

Extremely rare mail order ponies. M=$50, GR=$40, G=$30, P=$15

Dabble, light purple body, purple & blue mane, purple tail, purple & blue scribbles
Scribble, white body, pink and yellow mane, pink tail, pink & yellow scribbles

Pretty Pony

They look like Sweetheart Sisters, but they do not wear earrings. Their designs are in the shape of hearts. M=$6, GR=$5, G=$4, P=$1

Garden Glow, purple body, purple hair, pink heart with flowers inside
Rosy Love, pink body, pink hair, green heart with doves in it
Beautybloom, orange body, melon hair, blue heart box of candy
Flower Dream, blue body, blue hair, pink heart of flowers around a solid pink heart

Pretty Princess Ponies

Only 2 of these were made, and they were just called Pretty Princess Ponies. They all have rooted eyelashes and came with a silver tiara crown and shimmery fur trimmed cape. They are moderately hard to find. M=$15, GR=$10, G=$5, P=$1

Pretty Princess Ponies
Pretty Princess, Pink body, blue hair, castle
Pretty Princess, lavender body, pink hair, carriage

Pretty Princesses with their capes and crowns.

First Set – Group 1
  Princess Serena, light blue body, light pink hair/gold tinsel, heart jewel. Dark blue wand, purple hat w/hearts & tear drops and yellow ribbons, Bushwoolie: Cheerful, lt. pink, purple crown/pink diamond
  Princess Royal Blue, blue body, pink hair/pink tinsel, moon jewel/clear center. Purple wand, blue hat w/moons & stars and pink ribbons, Bushwoolie: Wishful, light pink, blue crown/pink circle
  Princess Starburst, yellow body, purple hair/silver tinsel, star jewel/yellow center. Pink wand, yellow hat w/moons & stars and pink ribbons, Bushwoolie: Sunny, purple, green crown/purple heart

Princess Ponies

There were two sets of Princess Ponies made, one in 1986 and one in 1987. The first set came with damsel hats, wands, and bushwoolies. The second set came with crowns that clipped in their hair, and wands. All have a jewel medallion affixed to each side of their rump for a design.

First Set: 1986

The cone hats have glittery shapes on them & ribbons trimmed in gold flowing from the tops. The wand color, hats & bushwoolies are listed after the pony's description. Ponies: M=$10, GR=$8, G=$6, P=$4, Bushwoolies: M=$10, GR=$8, G=$6, P=$3, Damsel Hats: M=$15, GR=$10, G=$8, P=$5, Wands: M=$10, GR=$8, G=$6, P=$4.

Second Set: 1987

Their wand and crown color/type are listed at the end of the descriptions. Ponies: M=$10, GR=$8, G=$6, P=$4, Crowns: M=$15, GR=$10, G=$8, P=$5, Wands: M=$10, GR=$8, G=$6, P=$4

First Set – Group 2

Princess Primrose, pink body, blue hair/pink tinsel, butterfly jewel/pink center. Purple wand, pink hat w/flowers & butterflies, yellow ribbons, Bushwoolie: Charmington, yellow, blue crown/circle

Princess Sparkle, unicorn, light purple body, light green hair/blue tinsel, star jewel. Pink wand, pink hat w/flowers & butterflies, yellow ribbons, Bushwoolie: Hugster, green, purple crown/diamond

Princess Tiffany, pegasus, white body, white hair/silver tinsel, teardrop jewel. Dark blue wand, purple hat w/hearts & tear drops & yellow ribbons, Bushwoolie: Friendly, lt. blue, purple crown/blue heart

Second Set

Princess Pristina, pegasus, green body, neon green hair/green tinsel, diamond/pink center. Pink wand, and dark pink diamond crown.

Princess Sunbeam, pink body, yellow hair/pink tinsel, circle jewel/ pink center. Yellow wand, and purple oval crown.

Princess Taffeta, blue body, white hair/rainbow tinsel, oval jewel/blue center. Yellow wand, and blue crown.

Princess Misty, purple body, pink hair/purple tinsel, oval jewel/pink center. Aqua wand, and blue crown.

Princess Moondust, yellow body, light pink hair/pink tinsel, crown-shaped jewel/gold center. Pink wand, and green crown.

Princess Dawn, light pink body, light purple hair/purple tinsel, tulip shaped jewel/pink center. Aqua wand, and yellow oval crown.

Prom Queen Sweetheart Sister Ponies

Like other Sweetheart Sisters, these gals have a flower earring. Each came with a pretty, flashy dress, a flower barrette, and a bottle of perfume. You can take off the dress and wear it in your hair. M=$8, GR=$6, G=$4, P=$2

Cha Cha, light yellow body, blue hair, pink bouquet, pink flower earring, light pink dress, purple barrette

Sweet Sundrop, pale pink body, light pink hair, tiara and stars, blue flower earring, pink dress, orange barrette

Daisy Dancer, blue body, purple hair, purple violin and music notes, pink flower earring, blue dress, yellow barrette

Pretty Belle, pink body, yellow hair, blue gloves and perfume bottle, lavender flower earring, yellow dress, blue barrette

Rainbow Ponies

Rainbow ponies have four different colors in their hair. This is what makes them Rainbow ponies. These ponies came out in two different groups. I have heard that they were available both through mail order and in stores.

Rainbow Ponies - Group 1. M=$15, GR=$10, G=$5, P=$1

Trickles, yellow/green body, melon/pink/blue/yellow hair, glittery copper watering can & drops

Flutterbye, pegasus, orange body, melon/pink/blue/yellow, glittery orange butterflies

Tickle, pegasus, purple body, melon/pink/blue/yellow hair, glittery gold feathers

Starflower, unicorn, blue body, melon/pink/blue/yellow hair, pink stars

Confetti, white body, melon/pink/blue/yellow, glittery red & green confetti

Pinwheel, unicorn, pink body, melon/pink/blue/yellow hair, glittery silver pinwheels

Rainbow Ponies - Group 2. M=$15, GR=$10, G=$5, P=$1

Moonstone, unicorn, light blue body, pink/yellow/green/blue hair, glittery sliver saturn/dots/planets

Sky Dancer, pegasus, yellow body, pink/yellow/green/blue hair, glittery blue birds

Star Shine, pegasus, white body, pink/yellow/green/blue hair, gold star

Sunlight, light blue body, pink/yellow/green/blue hair, silver glittery sun & gold glittery clouds

Windy, unicorn, light lavender, pink/yellow/green/blue hair, glittery purple wind swirl

Parasol, pale pink body, pink/yellow/green/blue hair, glittery pink umbrellas

Rainbow Curl Ponies

Each have four different colors of hair in four beautiful curled locks. Both their mane and tail are done this way. M=$6, GR=$5, G=$4, P=$1

Ringlet, pegasus, yellow body, white/yellow/pink/blue hair, wings are
    different colors and different colored stars down front leg
Rain Curl, white body, lt. pink/ yellow/purple/blue hair, cloud with rainbow
    tail purple stars and dots
Streaky, unicorn, purple body, pink/yellow/purple/deep melon hair, rainbow
    music staff with blue music notes and pink stars
Stripes, pastel pink body, pink/yellow/melon/blue hair, yellow stars on rump
    & down leg shooting star stripes from front shoulder back to star on rump

Regular Ponies

These were ponies that were made before all the fancy types were made. They were made from around 1983-1984. They are all fairly easy to find.

Earthlings (Ponies that don't have a horn or wings). M=$4, GR=$3, G=$2,
P=$1
    Cherries Jubilee, peach body, melon hair, cherries
    Tootsie, green body, blue hair, pink lollipops
    Lickety-Split, purple body, pink hair, ice cream cones
    Sea Shell, purple body, green hair, green sea shells - sitting pose!
    Bubbles, yellow body, blue hair, green bubbles - sitting pose!
    Posey, yellow body, pink hair, pale pink flowers
    Bow Tie, blue body, pink hair, pink bows, freckles
    Applejack, orange, yellow hair, red apples, freckles

Earthlings that came with a pony place or set:
  Sundance, white body, pink hair, pink heart circle. *See "Sundance Sets"*
  Lemon Drop, yellow body, purple hair, purple drops (Show Stable). *See "Ponies & Places."* Lemon Drop was reproduced as part of the five "Playset Ponies" available through mail order. The only difference found between the two Lemon Drops is how the information is arranged in her feet. The one that came with the Show Stable has info only in her front two feet. The Playset one has info in all four feet.
  Peachy, peach body, pink hair, pink hearts (Pretty Parlor). *See "Ponies & Places"*

Pegasus Ponies. M=$4, GR=$3, G=$2, P=$1
  Medley, pegasus, green body, green hair, green glittery music notes
  Firefly, pegasus, pink body, blue hair, blue glittery lightning bolts (positioned on toe)
  Surprise, pegasus, white body, neon green hair, purple glittery balloons
  Heart Throb, pegasus, light pink body, pink hair, pink hearts with glittery silver wings

These pegasus ponies were a part of sets & places.
  Sprinkles, pegasus, lavender body, blue hair, blue
    ducks (from the Waterfall) - "Ponies & Places."
    Sprinkles was also reproduced as one of the five
    "Playset Ponies." There is a major difference
    between the original Sprinkles and this one. The
    Waterfall Sprinkles has a lavender body and the
    Playset has a pink body!!
  Firefly, pegasus, pink body, blue hair, blue painted
    on lightning bolts - in standing pose. This one
    came with video, for more info check "Firefly
    and Video."

Unicorns. M=$4, GR=$3, G=$2, P=$1
  Twilight, unicorn, pink body, white hair with purple stripe in mane,
    glittery purple stars
  Gusty, unicorn, white body, green hair, red stripe in mane, glittery
    purple leaves
  Sparkler, unicorn, light blue, purple hair, red stripe in mane, blue
    glittery diamonds
  Glory, unicorn, white body, purple hair, blue stripe in mane, glittery
    blue and purple shooting star

Sunbeam, unicorn, light blue, white hair, yellow stripe in mane,
    glittery gold sun on side
Powder, unicorn, purple body, white hair, red stripe in mane, glittery
    silver snow flakes
Moon Dancer, unicorn, white body, red hair, purple stripe in mane,
    glittery purple moon & red stars
Skyflier, unicorn, orange body, red hair, white stripe in mane, purple
    glittery kites

Unicorn that came with a place or in a set.
  Majesty, unicorn, white body, blue hair, blue sparkly blossoms
    (Dream Castle)- "Ponies & Places." Majesty was also repro-
    duced to go with a set of five ponies called the "Playset Ponies."
    No differences can be seen between the original and the
    reproduced one.

Rockin' Beat Ponies

Each is neon-colored with very neon, crimped hair. Each came with a neon-colored guitar brush, if they have their brush add $2. M=$6, GR=$5, G=$4, P=$1

Tunefull, unicorn, blue body, red hair, purple mane stripe, pink & orange squares all over - pink brush

Pretty Beat, purple body, blue hair, orange mane stripe, red & yellow shapes all over - yellow brush

Sweet Notes, pink body, neon green hair, pink mane stripe, multicolored designs all over - orange brush

Half Note, orange body, pink hair, yellow mane stripe, neon green & pink shapes all over - lime green

Scrub-a-Dub Tub Gift Pack Ponies

See "Gift Packs & Sets" for values of the whole set with accessories. M=$5, GR=$4, G=$3, P=$2

Sunny Bunch, purple body, green hair, white/pink flower saddle - Merry-Go-Round Pony

Spring Song, purple body, purple hair, yellow flower bouquet - Sweetheart Sister Pony

Sky Rocket, blue body, red hair, rocket - Sparkle Pony

Sea Ponies

These were the first Sea Ponies made. They have a weight in their tail to make them stand straight in the water. Each came in a shell with a suction cup to adhere it to the bathtub. With shell add $2 to value. There was a set of three made (shown), then a set of six (not shown).

Sea Ponies - Set of 3. M=$6, GR=$5, G=$4, P=$1

Wavedancer, pink body, blue hair, lavender clam shell

Sea Winkle, blue body, lavender hair, pink clam shell

Sea Light, purple body, pink hair, green clam shell

Not shown: Sea Ponies - *Set of 6.* M=$10, GR=$8, G=$6, P=$3.

High Tide, yellow body, pink hair, lavender clam shell;

Sand Dollar, pink body, green hair, green clam shell;

Wave Jumper, blue body, pink hair, green clam shell;

Sea Mist, white body, red hair pink stripe, fushia cockle/twisted shell;

Whitecap, white body, purple hair blue stripe, pink cockle/twisted shell;

Sea Breeze, purple body, purple hair green stripe, blue cockle/twisted shell

Secret Surprise Beauties

These ponies have backs/saddles that open up only when you insert the key into the key hole on their neck and turn it. If the pony is missing their saddle, then they are not considered mint. For every item they have, (e.g., key or comb), add $2 to their value. M=$8, GR=$6, G=$4, P=$2

Secret Beauty, blue body, purple mane, white saddle that opens: purple hearts, came w/comb, key, & ring

Secret Star, purple body, pink hair, pink saddle that opens: yellow stars

Pretty Puff, white body, pink hair, light green saddle that opens: pink hearts/pink & purple trim

Stardazzle, pink body, aqua hair, purple saddle that opens: blue stars

So Soft Ponies

So Softs have a fuzzy, flocked finish. This makes them feel ever so soft to the touch! They came in a group of 6 and a group of 21.

So Softs - Group 1. M=$8, GR=$6, G=$4, P=$2
Crumpet, yellow body, gold hair, purple teapot and cup
Twilight, pegasus, purple body, pink hair, candle in holder. Twilight is hard to find. M=$12, GR=$10, G=$6, P=$3
Hippity Hop, pegasus, light purple body, pink hair, white bunnies
Angel, green body, blue hair, pink fish with blue stripes
Taffy, white body, pink hair, pink candies(taffy)
Bangles, unicorn, pink body, blue hair, pink stripe in mane, red heart with pearl necklace

So Softs - Group 2. M=$8, GR=$6, G=$4, P=$2
Posey, yellow body, pink hair, pink flowers(tulips)
Magic Star, yellow body, green hair, pink/green wand. She is in a raring pose!
Lickety-Split, pink body, pink hair, purple/white ice cream cones
Cup Cake, white body, blue hair, cup cakes
Scrumptious, white body, green hair, red & green watermelon slice
Shady, pink body, neon yellow hair, blue/white sunglasses
Truly, white body, pink hair, green dove with rose in beak. She is in a raring pose!
Skippity-Doo, green body, red hair, pink twisted jump rope. She is in a raring pose!
Cherries Jubilee, orange body, melon hair, green/red cherries

So Softs - Group 2, Continued
- Paradise, pegasus, white body, red hair, green palm trees
- Lofty, pegasus, yellow body, yellow hair, pink/orange hot air balloon
- Wind Whistler, pegasus, light blue body, pink hair, pink whistles
- Surprise, pegasus, white body, yellow hair, purple balloons
- North Star, pegusas, pink body, purple hair, purple/blue compass
- Bouncy, pegasus, yellow body, blue hair, beach ball
- Heart Throb, pegasus, light pink body, pink hair, pink hearts

So Softs - Group 2, Continued.
- Ribbon, unicorn, blue body, neon yellow hair, orange stripe in mane, white ribbon
- Buttons, unicorn, light pink body, blue hair, pink stripe in mane, pink buttons
- Twist, unicorn, purple body, orange hair/white mane stripe, white pretzels
- Gusty, unicorn, white body, green hair, red stripe in mane, purple leaves
- Fifi, unicorn, blue body, white hair, pink mane stripe, 3 pink poodles

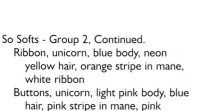

These So Softs were a part of a set.
- Sundance, white body, pink hair, pink circle of hearts. Came with Megan through mail offer. *See "Sundance Sets"*
- Best Wishes, pegasus, pink body, yellow hair, blue & white candles. Came with "Party Pack"

40

Sparkle Ponies (Store Versions)

A set was made for store sales and a set for mail order sales. Prices for the store versions: M=$6, GR=$5, G=$4, P=$1

Stardancer, purple body, blue hair/ pink tinsel, yellow and white stars

Sun Spot, orange body, orange hair/ gold tinsel, red sun

Star Hopper, unicorn, blue body, yellow hair/gold tinsel, pink UFO

Sky Rocket, blue body, red hair/blue tinsel, pink and purple rocket. Sky Rocket was reproduced as a part of the "Scrub-A-Dub Tub" gift pack. No differences can be seen between the two.

Napper, green body, purple hair/gold tinsel, green moon on purple cloud

Twinkler, pegasus, purple body, purple hair/rainbow tinsel, pink stars

Sparkle Ponies (Mail Order Versions)

A couple ponies had different hair colors and all ponies have a design on their cheek. M=$8, GR=$6, G=$4, P=$2.

Stardancer, purple body, blue hair/pink tinsel, yellow and white stars - yellow star on cheek

Sky Rocket, blue body, red hair/blue tinsel, pink and purple rocket - pink/purple rocket on cheek

Sun Spot, orange body, light pink hair/gold tinsel, red sun - yellow smiley face on cheek

Twinkler, pegasus, purple body, purple hair, pink stars. *Courtesy of Stephanie Stair*

Napper, green body, green hair/gold tinsel, green purple moon on cloud - purple cloud on cheek

Star Hopper, unicorn, blue body, white hair, pink UFO. Star Hopper is the hardest to find mail order sparkle pony. M=$15, GR=$12, G=$6, P=$2. *Courtesy of Linda Waite*

Special Pony

This special little pony was given out to children who had cancer. M=$15, GR=$12, G=$6, P=$2

Lil Tot, white body, dk pink hair, purple doll/blue ball/teddy bear

Summer Winged Ponies

These cute adults have delicate, flexible butterfly wings. M=$8, GR=$6, G=$4, P=$2

Lady Flutter, pink body, white hair, yellow lady bug, wing colors: yellow/pink/ green

Buzzer, green body, yellow hair, yellow bee, wing colors: dark pink/blue/yellow

High Flyer, light purple body, blue hair, silver dragon fly, wing colors: purple/ blue/yellow

Glow, blue body, light pink hair, pink firefly, wing colors: orange/pink/blue

Little Flitter, yellow body, light pink hair, magenta humming bird, wing colors: blue/yellow/purple

Sky Dancer, purple body, blue hair, white dove with rose, wing colors: green/pink/ yellow

Sundae Best Ponies

They all have a 3-D ice cream design. They are also scented like ice cream; you just want to eat them up! M=$5, GR=$4, G=$3, P=$2

Peppermint Crunch, pegasus, green body, purple hair, pink & white swirl ice cream cone

Coco Berry, unicorn, blue body, light pink hair, pink & yellow ice cream cone with sprinkles

Swirly Whirly, yellow body, gold hair, green & pink 3 scoop ice cream cone

Banana Surprise, pink body, blue hair, white & yellow banana split

Sherbert, purple body, pink hair, pink & white sundae

Crunch Berry, pink body, neon yellow hair, blue & white sundae with spoon

Sundance Sets

In each set Sundance came with a pink velvet bridle and Megan came in a dress, underwear, and pink shoes.

Original Sundance. Megan (Consider Megan's clothes): M=$6, GR=$5, G=$4, P=$3. Pony: M=$5, GR=$4, G=$3, P=$2. Set: M=$12, GR=$10, G=$8, P=$4

Sundance, white body, pink hair, pink circle of hearts.

Megan is blonde and wearing a white dress with pink lace and pink shoes.

So Soft Sundance (fuzzy!!). Megan (Consider Megan's clothes): M=$10, GR=$8, G=$5, P=$4. Pony: M=$8, GR=$6, G=$4, P=$2. Set: M=$25, GR=$20, G=$15, P=$6.

    Sundance, white body, pink hair, pink hearts in a circle

    Megan is blonde and wearing a colorful flower dress

Sunshine Sundance. This variation of Sundance resembles a Twice as Fancy by having her design all over her. Megan's and her hair turns from white to purple in the sun. Megan (Consider Megan's clothes): M=$10, GR=$8, G=$5, P=$4. Pony: M=$5, GR=$4, G=$3, P=$2. Set: M=$16, GR=$12, G=$8, P=$4.

    Sundance, white body, light pink /white hair, pink circle of hearts all over her

    Megan is blonde and wearing a white dress with hot pink trim, and Sundance's design all over it

Not Shown: Twice-As-Fancy Sundance. Sundance has her design all over her, but she is the same pose as original Sundance. Her hair does not change color! This is a harder to find set, especially Sundance. Megan (Consider Megan's clothes): M=$12, GR=$10, G=$6, P=$4. Pony: M=$18, GR=$15, G=$10, P=$4. Set: M=$35, GR=$30, G=$20, P=$10. Sundance, white body, pink hair, and has her circle of hearts design all over her. Megan is blonde and wearing a white dress with pink trim and Sundance's design all over it

Sun Shine Ponies

    Sunshine Ponies have a section of hair that changes color in the sun. They resemble Twice as Fancies by having their design all over their body. M=$6, GR=$5, G=$4, P=$1

Beach ball, unicorn, purple body, blue hair, white streak, beach balls and stars all over

Shoreline, purple body, white hair, light pink streak, suns with sun-glasses all over

Wave Runner, pegasus, pink body, green hair, white streak, sea horses and bubbles all over

Sea Flower, green body, blue hair, light pink streak, sea shells and pink star fish all over

Sand Digger, yellow body, light green hair, white streak, shovels and buckets all over

Main Sail, blue body, yellow hair, white streak, sail boats all over

A Sunshine Sundance was also made. *See "Sundance Sets."*

After exposure to sun, gorgeous deep colors appear in the hair.

Sweetberry Ponies

Each have a berry related design and even smell like berries! M=$6, GR=$5, G=$4, P=$1

Raspberry Jam, pink body, green hair, purple/white/yellow jar of jam

Cherry Treats, white body, red hair, blue/red/green bowl of cherries

Boysenberry Pie, unicorn, purple body, yellow hair, pink/yellow/purple slice of pie

Strawberry Surprise, orange body, pink hair, green/red/white bowl of strawberries & milk

Cranberry Muffins, green body, pink hair, blue/yellow/pink muffin and cranberries

Blueberry Baskets, pegasus, blue body, blue hair, orange/blue/green basket of blue berries

Sweetheart Sister Ponies

Each is wearing a flower earring. The earring color is listed at the end of the pony's description. M=$8, GR=$6, G=$4, P=$2

Flowerburst, blue body, blue hair, pink flowers with pink bow, pink flower earring

Spring Song, purple body, purple hair, yellow flowers with yellow bow, yellow flower. Spring Song was also reproduced as part of the Scrub -A- Dub Tub gift set. No changes can bee seen between the two.

Dainty, pink body, pink hair, purple flowers with purple bow, purple flower earring

Frilly Flower, yellow body, green hair, pink flowers with pink bow, pink flower earring

Fancy Flower, light green body, pink hair , pink flowers with pink bow, melon flower earring

Wild Flower, orange body, orange hair, blueberries with blue bow, blue flower earring

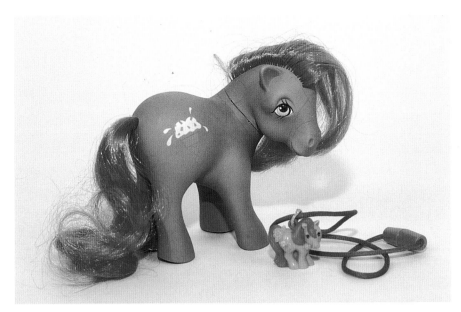

Sweet Scoops & Pendant

Available through mail order only, this pony came with a pony pendant on an necklace for you to wear. M (w/pendant)=$35, GR (no pendent)=$30, G=$15, P=$5

Sweet Scoops, purple body, purple hair, purple & white ice cream cone.

Sweetsteps Ballerinas

Each are wearing molded on body suits and slippers. Be careful when determining body color, their body is color is the color of their legs and head. M=$6, GR=$5, G=$4, P=$1

Tip Toes, purple body, green suit, yellow hair, pink flowers

Silky Slipper, pink body, purple suit, blue hair, pink ballet slippers and stars

Twinkle Dancer, yellow body, pink suit, purple hair, blue fan

Posey Rose, blue body, yellow suit, pink hair, pink music notes and staff

10th Anniversary Ponies

These were the last ponies produced by Hasbro in 1991. They are to celebrate 10 years of pony making. The first pony was made in 1981! M=$15, GR=$12, G=$6, P=$2

Birthday Pony: white body, pink hair/ blue tinsel & curly ribbon in her tail, party decorations all over

Colorswirl: Springy, pink and white striped body, purple & white hair, blue coil in a box

Colorswirl: Love Beam, orange and white striped body, blue & pink hair, pink hat in a box

Colorswirl: Starswirl, blue & purple striped body, pink & blue hair, white heart in a box

Sippin' Soda: Chocolate Delight, pink body, blue/pink/yellow hair, chocolate soda float, came with a soda she sips

Sippin' Soda: Strawberry Scoops, purple body, pink/blue/white hair, strawberry soda float, came with soda she sips

Flower Fantasy: Sweet Blossom, pink body white flowers all over her, blue hair, yellow flower bouquet

Flower Fantasy: Flowerbelle, purple body w/blue flowers all over her, pink hair, 2 pink interlocked hearts

Flower Fantasy: Lovepetal, white body w/ purple flowers all over her, purple hair, blue placemat w/hearts

Sweet Kisses (Sweetheart Sister): Happy Hugs, pink body, blue hair/ blue tinsel, purple lips and lip stick, her lips turn red with cold water.

Sweet Kisses (Sweetheart Sister): Ruby Lips, blue body, purple hair/ purple tinsel, pink lips & XOs, her lips turn pink with cold water.

Sweet Kisses (Sweetheart Sister): Lovin' Kisses, white body, pink hair/ pink tinsel, blue X, O, & hearts, her lips turn pink with cold water.

Sundazzle (Sweetheart Sister): Sun Glory, yellow body, white/blue/tan hair, white turns pink in sun, pink & purple beach umbrella

Sundazzle (Sweetheart Sister): Sunsplasher, orange body, tan/purple/white hair, white turns pink in sun, yellow sun with sunglasses

Sundazzle (Sweetheart Sister): Sunbeam, hot pink body, white/yellow/tan hair, white turns pink in sun, sun with sailboat and palm trees

Sweet Talkin' Pony: pink body, pink hair, ponies talking. Squeeze her rump and she says three things, "I'm Pretty," "I love You," and "Comb My Hair." Replaceable batteries in neck, twist-off head

Sweet Talkin' Pony: purple body, purple hair, ponies on a telephone. Squeeze her rump and she says three things, "I'm Pretty," "I love You," and "Comb My Hair." Batteries are replaceable.

Wedding Pony: Bridle Beauty, white body, white hair/silver tinsel, pink heart & bouquet of roses

Tropical Ponies
Very colorful ladies to decorate your tropical party! M=$6, GR=$5, G=$4, P=$1

Hula Hula, unicorn, purple body, neon orange/red/green hair, green & orange striped sailboat

Tootie Tails, yellow body, neon yellow/green/pink hair, pink pineapple

Pina Colada, pink body, neon orange/red/blue hair, blue & orange palm trees

Sea Breeze, pegasus, orange body, pink/neon yellow/red hair, pink & blue striped fish

Twice As Fancy Ponies
These gals came in two different groups. M=$6, GR=$5, G=$4, P=$1

Twice as Fancies - Group 1. M=$15, GR=$12, G=$6, P=$2

Sweet Tooth, blue body, pink hair, purple and pink lollipops all over her

Up Up and Away, pink body, pink hair, green and yellow balloons all over her

Milky Way, unicorn, pink body, white hair with blue stripe in mane, silver stars all over her

Dancing Butterflies, pegasus, yellow body, yellow hair, pink and blue butterflies all over

Sugarberry, white body, red hair, strawberries all over attached to a vine

Love Melody, purple body, pink hair, hearts all over attached to a string

Twice as Fancies - Group 2. M=$15, GR=$12, G=$6, P=$2

Munchy, yellow body, melon hair, brown/green hot dogs and hamburgers all over her

Night Glider, blue body, white hair, stars and planets all over her

Merriweather, purple body, yellow hair, rainbows all over her

Yum Yum, pegasus, white body, pink hair, pink candy all over her

Buttons, unicorn, green body, blue hair, white buttons and pink bows all over her

Bonnie Bonnets, pink body, white hair, yellow and blue hats all over her

47

Twice as Fancies that were a part of a place or set.

- Scoops, white body, purple hair, soda floats all over (Satin Slipper Sweet Shoppe). *See "Ponies & Places"*
- Pillow Talk, grayish body, yellow/blue/white hair, white pillows/yellow moons all over. See *"Slumber Party Pack"*
- Fifi, white body, blue hair, pink bows all over (Perm Shoppe). *See "Ponies & Places"*
- Sundance, white body, pink hair, and has her circle of hearts design all over her. *See "Sundance Sets"*

Twinkle Eyed Ponies

Twinkle eyes have sparkly gems in their eyes! These ponies came in two different groups.

Twinkle Eyed - Group 1. M=$15, GR=$12, G=$6, P=$2

- Mimic, unicorn, light green body, yellow/light pink/green/red hair, red parrot
- Locket, pegasus, pink body, white/pink/melon/light purple hair, pink & purple keys
- Quackers, white body, blue/green/yellow/pink hair, yellow duck with umbrella
- Tic Tac Toe, yellow body, red/pink/blue/green hair, green & yellow tic tac toe board
- Speedy, unicorn, orange body, blue/white/yellow/purple hair, white roller skates
- Bright Eyes, blue, white/yellow/orange/red hair, red alarm clock

Twinkle Eyed – Group. 2 M=$15, GR=$12, G=$6, P=$2

- Galaxy, unicorn, purple body, red/white/pink/orange hair, dipper of pink stars
- Sky Rocket, purple body, red/yellow/white/light pink hair, red fire work blasts
- Fizzy, unicorn, green body, light pink/white/pink/green hair, pink milk shakes
- Sweet Stuff, light blue body, light purple/pink/light pink/white hair, pink & purple gum drops

Gingerbread, white body, blue/purple/white/light purple hair, blue ginger bread men
Sweet Pop, pegasus, blue body, pink/yellow/light purple/light pink, pink twin-pop popsicles
Masquerade, pegasus, yellow body, green/blue/light green/yellow hair, green & pink masks
Whizzer, pegasus, light pink body, dark purple/blue/green/light blue hair, pink beanies

This pony was part of the "Party Pack." Party Time, orange body, white/yellow/ blue hair, party hats.

Wedding Couple

This cute couple was only available through the mail. Satin 'n Lace came three different ways and her stallion came with two different names. He had the name Coat 'n Tails when sold separately from Satin 'n Lace in 1988, and the name Tux 'n Tails when sold with Satin 'n Lace as a set in 1990. Individually: M=$30, GR=$25, G=$15, P=$8

Satin 'n Lace & Tux 'n Tails

Satin 'n Lace in her wedding outfit.

Satin 'n Lace, (So Soft), light purple, pink hair, blue wedding bells, came with wedding dress, garter, ring, veil, and four white bow shoes. (1986). *Photo courtesy of Beckie Bassett*

Not shown: Satin 'n Lace, (standing), pink body, pink hair, wedding bells wedding dress/veil/ garter/ring/white bow shoes (1987)

Not shown: Coat 'n Tails, big brother, blue body, blue hair, white bowties, came with blue bowtie (came out in 1988)

Not shown: Satin 'n Lace, (walking/moving), light purple body, pink hair, wedding bells, wedding dress/veil/garter/ring/ white bow shoes (1988)

Not shown: Tux 'n Tails, big brother, blue body, blue hair, white bows, came with blue bow tie, (came out in 1990)

Wedding Pony

Came out the same time as Promqueens. She came in a half circle type box with a see-through front. This is the only Wedding Pony that was made. She is a fairly common pony. M=$6, GR=$5, G=$4, P=$1

Dum Dum de Dum, white body, white hair/white tinsel, two purple doves tying a blue ribbon with wedding rings on it. She came with a veil, ring and a wedding cake.

Windy Winged Ponies

They resemble Summer Wings, but have totally different designs and wings are shaped differently. M=$10, GR=$8, G=$6, P=$4.

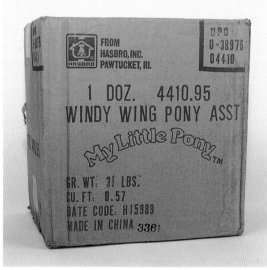

Flurry, purple body, light pink hair, white snow flake, wing colors: green/blue/pink

Sun Glider, pink body, blue hair, yellow sun behind clouds, wing colors: yellow/pink/purple

Cool Breeze, light green body, green hair, palm tree, wing colors: green/blue/pink

Starry Wings, yellow body, dark pink hair, blue moon and stars, wing colors: pink/purple/yellow

Moon Jumper, lt. pink body, blue hair, cow jumping over a moon, wing colors: yellow/purple/blue

Whirly, blue body, yellow hair, sun, wing colors: yellow/pink/blue

Someone mailed me ponies in this original Hasbro shipping box for Windy Wings!

Snail rockers, baby rockers, baby diapers with boxes, stack toys, duck pull toys, wagons, baby necklaces, bottles, cribs, highchair, xylophone, divided dish with spoon, blankets, and bassinets.

Babies came with a variety of baby toys and accessories, including snail rockers, baby rockers, baby diapers with boxes, stack toys, duck pull toys, wagons, baby necklaces, bottles, cribs, highchair, xylophone, divided dish with spoon, blankets, and bassinets. Keep an eye out for all of these items as you search through toy bins! All pictures read left to right and front to back. Babies are valued at these values unless otherwise noted:

Mint Condition(M) no hair trims or permanent marks

Great Condition(GR) a couple minor unnoticeable marks, tiny hair snip

Good Condition(G) permanent marks, hair trims, not to bad

Poor(P) really bad off, many marks, hair cut.

Babies with Baby Buggies

These two babies came with their vary own baby buggy. For value of complete set and contents check under "Gift Packs & Sets."

Baby Cuddles (Beddy-Bye-Eyed), light blue, pink hair, rattle. Her set is called "Baby Cuddles and Baby Buggy." M=$5, GR=$4, G=$3, P=$2

Princess Sparkle, gold glittery star on forehead, white body, pink hair with tinsel, glittery castle in clouds. Her set is called "Princess and Baby Buggy." M=$15, GR=$10, G=$5, P=$2

Baby Blue Ribbon & Game

Baby Blue Ribbon came with a game for you and your ponies to play, and she gets to award the winning pony with a blue ribbon. Baby Blue Ribbon's game is called "Adventures in Ponyland" and it came with: Baby Blue Ribbon, blue ribbon prize, cardboard die, and game board. "Adventure" cards were available in pony packages to go along with the game. *Very rare set*: M=$115, GR=$90, G=$45, P=$25, Pony: M=$55, GR=$50, G=$25, P=$15, Game: M=$50, GR=$45, G=$25, Poor=$10

Baby Blue Ribbon, blue body, blue hair, 1st place ribbon - I think she was a pony fan club exclusive.

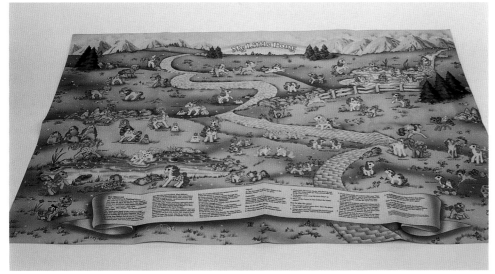

Blue Ribbon's Game (front).
Courtesy of Beckie Bassett

Baby Blue Ribbon's Game (back)

Baby Ember

Mail Order Versions! She is a very special pony, available through mail order only. She came in three different color combinations, each without a design. M=$5, GR=$4, G=$3, P=$2

Baby Ember, blue body, blue hair
Baby Ember, purple body, pink hair
Baby Ember, pink body, purple hair

Listen 'n Fun Version! Baby Ember came with a cassette called "Embers Dream" and has a white star design. M=$15, GR=$10, G=$5, P=$4
   Baby Ember, lavender body, lavender hair, white star

Baby Pony and Pretty Pal

These baby ponies came with an animal friend, I will describe the baby pony first then their friend. M=$5, GR=$4, G=$3, P=$2, Set: M=$15, GR=$10, G=$7, P=$5

Baby Lucky Leaf & Baby Leafy (cow). Baby Lucky Leaf, unicorn, yellow body, orange hair, clovers and flowers; Baby Leafy: orange body, yellow hair, clovers and leafs

Baby Pockets & Baby Hoppy (Kangeroo). Baby Pockets, pegasus, green body, pink hair, pockets with stuff in them; Baby Hoppy: pink body, green hair, pockets with stuff in them

Baby Fleecy & Baby Woolly (sheep). Baby Fleecy: pink body, pink hair, balls of yarn; Baby Woolly:, pink body, purple hair, balls of yarn

Baby Stripes & Baby Nectar (bear): Baby Stripes: blue body, white hair, bees; Baby Nectar: white & blue body, white hair, bees

Baby Pony Friends

Both Baby Pony Sets were made in 1987, and yes, I did say babies! The pony friends are really babies. Look at the quotes from the two different packages below. M=$15, GR=$10, G=$8, P=$5

Creamsicle, Spunky, Cha Cha, Oakly, Kingsley, Cutesaurus, Edgar, and Zig Zag

Set I. On package it says: "Baby animal friends for all your ponies!"
Baby Creamsicle, giraffe, yellow body, white hair, pink leaves.
Baby Zig Zag, zebra, pink body, pink hair, green stripes.
Baby Spunky, camel, blue body, purple hair, yellow triangles.
Baby Kingsley, lion, pink body, pink hair, blue paw prints.
Not Shown: Baby Sundance, baby pony, white body, pink hair, circle of hearts - has a First Tooth!!

Set II. On package it says: "Baby animal pals for your ponies!"
Baby Creamsicle, giraffe, yellow body, white hair, pink leaves.
Baby Kingsley, lion, pink body, pink hair, blue paw prints.
Baby Edgar, elephant, purple body, orange hair, blue peanuts.
Baby Cutesaurus, dinosaur, orange body, green hair, blue bones.
Baby Oakly, moose, pink body, blue hair, blue leaves.
Baby Cha Cha, llama, green body, pink baskets. *Cha Cha Courtesy of Stephanie Stair.*

Baby Pony with Purse

There were two different purses made, a pink and a purple, for young girls to carry. These purses are made from a soft canvas with a pillow/lace trimmed top that opens and closes. The cutest part is the little pocket on the front for baby to ride in. Purse & baby: M=$25, GR=$20, G=$15, P=$5

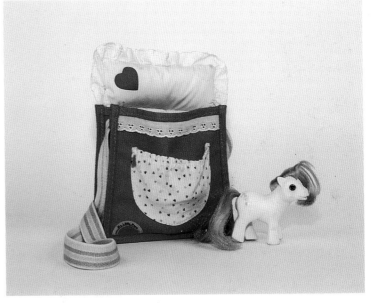

Purple Purse came with Baby Crumpet, yellow body, yellow hair, purple tea pot and cup - First Tooth, Crumpet: M=$15, GR=$12, G=$10, P=$5. *Purse, Courtesy of Stephanie Stair*

Pink Purse came with Baby Sleepy Pie, white, blue hair, teddy bear wearing night cap - Beddy-Bye-Eyed, Sleepy Pie: M=$5, GR=$4, G=$3, P=$2

Baby Sisters
Mail Order Only! Very Rare!! Each: M= $50, GR=$40, G=$25, P=$15

Li'l Sweetcake, unicorn, blue body, pink hair, white cake. She is a Peek-a-Boo baby.
Li'l Cupcake, unicorn, pink body, blue hair, pink and white cup cake. She is a Newborn Baby.

Ballerina Babies
They wear colored body suits, but do not have a design. They also have molded on ballet slippers. The body color is the same as their legs and head. M=$5, GR=$4, G=$3, P=$2

Toe Dancer, pink body suit, yellow
  body, purple hair
Tippy Toes, purple body suit, blue
  body, light pink hair
Sweetsteps, yellow body suit,
  lavender body, dark pink hair
Soft Steps, yellow body suit, pink
  body, green hair

Beddy-Bye-Eyed Babies
These little ones are so adorable! If you lay them down their eyes close, pick them up and their eyes open again. M=$5, GR=$4, G=$3, P=$2

Heart-Throb, pegasus, light pink body, pink
  hair, pink hearts, yellow playpen/pink
  heart blanket
Lofty, pegasus, light yellow body, yellow
  hair, pink hot air balloon, blue wagon
Shady, pink body, neon yellow hair,
  sunglasses, lavender highchair
Lickety-Split, pink body, pink hair, purple &
  white ice cream cones, yellow highchair
Ribbon, unicorn, blue body, yellow hair
  orange stripe, white bow, pink wagon
Gusty, unicorn, white body, green hair/red
  stripe, purple leaves, pink playpen/
  purple star blanket

These babies all came with a place or set.

Half Note, light purple body, blue hair, ballet slippers (Bonnet School of Dance). See "Ponies & Places"

Frosting, unicorn, green body, white hair, yellow party hats. See "Party Pack"

Tiddly Winks, light purple body, pink hair, white bib (Lullabye Nursery). See "Ponies & Places"

Sundance, white body, pink hair, pink hearts in a circle. See "Molly and Baby Sundance"

Cuddles, light blue body, pink hair, rattle. See "Baby and Baby Buggy"

Sleepy Pie, white body, blue hair, teddy bear. See "Baby Pony and Purse"

Chuck E Cheese Baby

She was only available as a prize at various Chuck E Cheeses. M=$10, GR=$8, G=$5, P=$2

Chuck E Cheese, purple with blue hair, Chuck E Cheese logo with "Chuck E Cheese" below it.

Drink 'n Wet Baby Ponies

Each baby came with changing table, two diapers, brush, ribbon, and bottle. Add $2 for each item they have in addition to the brush and ribbon. I have listed the color of their changing table last. M=$5, GR=$4, G=$3, P=$2

Cuddles, white body, gold hair, pink watering can and flower; lavender changing table

Flicker, yellow body, pink hair, fish bowl with fish; blue changing table

Rainfeather, pink body, blue hair, blue duck with umbrella & waters drops; yellow changing table

Snookums, unicorn, purple body, light pink hair, yellow hat and boots; green changing table

Fancy Pants Babies

Fancy Pants have painted-on diapers with designs on them. Each came with a dish and spoon, stack or pull toy, and sipper cup. M=$5, GR=$4, G=$3, P=$2

Baby Glider, unicorn, purple body, white hair/neon yellow bangs, green & pink butterflies

Baby Sunnybunch, green body, yellow hair/pink bangs, purple flowers

Baby Bows, blue body, white hair, pink & yellow bows

Baby Dots 'n Hearts, pegasus, purple body, green hair/white bangs, pink hearts and dots

Baby Splashes, yellow body, purple hair, blue ducks

Baby Starburst, pink body, blue hair, yellow & blue moons & stars

Came in a special mail order Mom & Baby set. *See "Mommy and Baby" for her value.*
Beachy Keen, purple body, pink hair, white painted on diaper w/hearts and baby cat

First Boy Babies

First Boy Baby Ponies, Mail Order Only! Very Rare!

Little Clipper, blue body, white hair, white & red sail boat. He is ready to set sails. M= $40, GR=$30, G=$20, P=$10

Lucky, blue body, blue hair, purple horse shoe. The first boy pony. M= $20, GR=$15, G=$10, P=$5

First Tooth Baby Ponies

Each little baby has a first tooth! M=$5, GR=$4, G=$3, P=$2

Baby Quackers, white body, blue/green/yellow/pink hair, yellow duck with umbrella

Baby Fifi, blue body, white hair, pink stripe in mane, pink poodles

Baby Lickety-Split, pink body, pink hair, purple and white ice cream cones

Baby North Star, pegasus, pink body, purple hair, purple compass

Baby Bouncy, pegasus, yellow body, blue hair, beach ball

Baby Tic Tac Toe, yellow body, red/pink/green/light green hair, tic tac toe board

These babies were a part of different sets.

Baby Night Cap, yellow body, pink hair, night caps - see "Slumber Party Gift Pack"

Baby Crumpet, yellow body, yellow hair, purple tea pot and cup - see "Baby Pony with Purse"

Not shown: Baby Sundance, white body, pink hair, pink hearts in a circle - see " Baby Pony Friends"

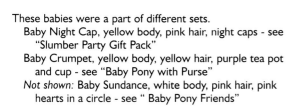

Kellogg's Christmas Baby

Kellogg's mail order special. Poor dear *didn't* come with a name so I gave it one! Everyone seems to call her Baby Stockings on the Internet, so that is what I named her. M=$5, GR=$4, G=$3, P=$2

Baby Stockings, white body, red hair, green stocking

Molly and Baby Sundance

Beddy-Bye-Eyed Baby Sundance was put with Megan's sister "Molly" to make this cute set! Molly is really hard to find, especially with all her clothes. Sundance came with a little pink velvet bridle just like her mom's. Set: M (Molly with all her clothes, Sundance with bridle)=$25, GR=$20, G=$15, P=$10. Molly: M (with all her clothes)=$20, GR (most of clothes)=$15, G (clothes missing)=$10, P=$5, Sundance: M= $5, GR=$4, G=$3, P=$2.

Baby Sundance, white body, pink hair, pink circle of hearts
- Beddy-Bye-Eyed
Molly is wearing a pink dress, striped tights, white shoes with hearts, and has hair in doggie tails.

Newborn Twins

Below is a list of their names with some items they came with, but they may not be correct. All came with 2 white bottles and 2 diapers with boxes (add $1 for each item they have). As for the other toys I am not sure on, *see "Came With" section for some toys.* Each: M=$5, GR=$4, G=$3, P=$2, Set: M=$12, GR=$10, G=$8, P=$6

1986 Nibbles & Dibbles - aqua bassinet w/pink hood
1986 Jangles & Tangles - snail rockers (blue & pink)
1986 Tattles & Rattles - stroller
1986 Doodles & Noodles - snail rockers (aqua & yellow)
1986 Sniffles & Snookums - blue/yellow covered stroller
1986 Tumbleweed & Milkweed - purple bassinet/yellow hood
1987 Shovels & Sandcastle - snail rockers (pink & yellow)
1987 Sticky & Sniffles - snail rockers (green & purple)
1987 Bunkie & Speckles - rattles, blanket, crib
1987 Big Top & Toppy - yellow sandbox
1987 Peeks & Puddles - blue/pink seesaw,
1987 Jabber & Jebber - dish/spoons, a pink & a purple necklace

Newborn Twins - 1986
  Nibbles, pegasus, pink body, orange hair, swan
  Dibbles, pegasus, orange body, pink hair, swan
  Jangles, light green body, yellow hair, white Humpty Dumpty,
  Tangles, light green body, white hair, white Humpty Dumpty,
  Tattles, unicorn, white body, right leg forward, head turned, yellow hair, yellow bunny
  Rattles, unicorn, white body, left leg forward, head turned, yellow hair, yellow bunny
  Doodles, pink body, pink hair, A B C
  Noodles, blue body, blue hair, A B C
  Sniffles, unicorn, light purple body, pink hair, pink mittens
  Snookums, unicorn, pink body, purple hair, purple mittens
  Tumbleweed, yellow body, looking straight ahead, pink hair, pink rocking horse
  Milkweed, yellow body, head tilted, pink hair, pink rocking horse

Newborn Twins - 1987

Shovels, unicorn, light blue body, yellow hair, orange sandcastle and shovel

Sandcastle, unicorn, orange body, blue hair, orange sandcastle and shovel

Sticky, pink body, white hair, blue horsehead with bridle

Sniffles, pink body, blue hair, blue horsehead with bridle

Bunkie, yellow body, purple hair, orange & blue safety pins - she rares!!

Speckles, light pink body, yellow hair, orange & blue safety pins - she rares!!

Toppy, white body, yellow hair, yellow doll,

Big Top, yellow body, white hair, yellow doll

Peeks, blue body, standing, head to left, purple hair, blue bird

Puddles, blue body, kneeling, purple hair, blue bird

Jabber, unicorn, light green body, right leg back, light pink hair, pink top

Jebber, unicorn, light green body, right leg forward, light pink hair, pink top

This set of twins came with the "Slumber Party Gift Pack."

Sleepy Head, light blue body, pink & blue striped pajamas

Sleep Tight, pink body, blue hair, yellow crib

Original Newborns

Set of six newborn babies, the first newborns made. M=$5, GR=$4, G=$3, P=$2

Baby Dangles, white body, blue hair, yellow/blue hanging mobile

Baby Wiggles, unicorn, green body, white hair, white/pink worms

Baby Squirmy, yellow body, green hair, green/pink snail

Baby Yo-Yo, pegasus, purple body, light pink hair, yo-yo - she rares!!

Baby Tappy, pink body, yellow hair, yellow/blue shoes

Baby Shaggy, blue body, pink hair, teddy bear doing handstand

Li'l Cupcake, unicorn, pink body, blue hair, pink and white cupcake. This baby is a part of the "Baby Sisters" set.

Party Babies

Mail Order Only! Very Rare! Came with Pin the Tail on the Pony game, 2 tails, one blind fold, slice of cake, candle, plate, & party favor. The ultimate party crew. M= $30, GR=$25, G=$20, P=$10

Baby Sugar Cake, pink body, yellow hair, pink stripe, blue balloon dog.
Baby Game Time, yellow body, pink hair, blue stripe, pink balloon dog.

Pearlized Baby Ponies

Mail Order Only! Baby Moondancer was renamed to Baby Moondreamer on all the order pamphlets for the pearlized babies. All are very rare! M= $25, GR=$20, G= $15, P=$5

Baby Blossom, purple body, white hair, white blossoms

Baby Glory, unicorn, blue body, purple hair, purple/blue shooting star

Baby Cotton Candy, pink body, pink hair, white specks

Baby Firefly, pegasus, pink body, blue hair, blue lightning bolt

Baby Moondreamer, unicorn, white body, magenta hair, purple moon & 2 magenta stars

Baby Surprise, pegasus, yellow body, yellow hair, purple balloon

Peek-A-Boo Babies

All came with a little bib tied around their necks; heads swivel. M=$5, GR=$4, G=$3, P=$2

Graffiti, pegasus, (has tooth), white body, blue hair, crayons
Snippy, yellow body, pink hair, two pink cut outs and scissors
Noddins, unicorn, purple body, white hair, purple bunny
Whirly Twirl, (Baby Big Brother), pink body, green hair, yellow helicopter
Ribs, (Baby Big Brother), green body, green hair, purple dragon
Sweet Stuff, (has tooth)pink body, pink hair, blue doll

This baby is a part of the "Baby Sisters" set. Li'l Sweetcake, unicorn, blue body, pink hair, white cake.

Playtime Baby Brother Ponies

Each came with a neck scarf and toys. Their heads swivel and they have cute freckles. They look like Baby Big Brothers! M=$5, GR=$4, G=$3, P=$2

Racer, yellow body, blue hair, race car
Leaper, green body, yellow hair, frog
Drummer, blue body, melon hair, drum
Paws, green body, pink hair, scottie dog
Countdown, pink body, purple hair, rocket ship
Waddles, purple body, green hair, penguin

Pretty 'n Pearly Baby Sea Ponies

Have a pearly looking finish. Add $2 if they have their float. M=$5, GR=$4, G=$3, P=$2

Beachcomber, aqua body, blue hair, pink/green alligator float
Water Lily, pink body, green hair, pink/green frog float
Sun Shower, yellow body, gold hair, lt. blue/yellow alligator float
Ripple, white body, pink hair, green/pink frog float
Surf Rider, purple body, pink hair, blue/purple fish float
Sea Shimmer, green body, blue hair, purple/green turtle float

Baby Celebrate, white body, purple hair - purple/orange turtle float. This sea baby is a part of the "Party Pack."

Rainbow Baby Ponies

They have rainbow colored hair and related designs. M=$5, GR=$4, G=$3, P=$2

Sunribbon, green body, orange/yellow/green hair, rainbow on cloud, stars around

Brightbow, pegasus, pink body, blue/yellow/purple hair, rainbow with moon & stars

Rainribbon, unicorn, purple body, pink/yellow/blue hair, rainbow with sun behind cloud

Starbow, white body, pink/blue/yellow hair, rainbow with stars

Regular Babies

Most of these were featured in the movies and videos. The regular six came with toys, each came with a diaper, bib and bottle. I am not sure what toys or accessories came with who. M=$5, GR=$4, G=$3, P=$2

Surprise, pegasus, white body, yellow hair, glittery purple balloon

Cotton Candy, earthling, pink body, pink hair, white specks - lavender playpen/pink heart blanket

Firefly, pegasus, pink body, blue hair, blue glittery lightning bolts - baby necklace

Blossom, earthling, light purple body, white hair, 3 white flowers, freckles - blue rocker

Glory, unicorn, white body, purple hair blue stripe in mane, glittery purple shooting star

Moondancer, unicorn, white body, pink hair purple stripe in mane, pink glittery stars and moon

These three Earthlings came with various sets and places. Only two are shown here.

Cuddles, light blue body, pink hair, rattle, freckles (the Baby Buggy set)

Tiddly Winks, pink body, pink hair, white bib, has freckles (Lullabye Nursery). See "Ponies & Places"

Not shown: Tiddly Winks, pink body, pink hair, white bib, no freckles. See "Playset Ponies"

Not shown: Half-Note, purple body, blue mane, ballet slippers, has freckles (School of Dance). See "Ponies & Places"

Not shown: Half-Note, purple body, blue mane, ballet slippers, no freckles. See "Playset Ponies"

Regular Baby Sea Ponies
If they have their float add $2 to value. M=$5, GR=$4, G=$3, P=$2

Splasher, blue/green body, purple hair, green/blue turtle float
Backstroke, pink body, orange hair, blue/orange fish float
Sea Shimmer, green body, blue hair, pink/green turtle float
Surf Rider, pink body, pink hair, blue/purple fish float
Sea Star, yellow body, purple hair, pink/blue duck float
Tiny Bubbles, light blue body, yellow hair, yellow/orange duck float

Sea Sparkle Baby Sea Ponies
Each are wearing a painted on seashell necklace and pendant listed at the end of their descriptions. If they have the float add $2 to value. M=$5, GR=$4, G=$3, P=$2

Sea Breeze, green body, yellow hair, pink stripe, pink/purple lobster float, pink scallop shell
Dipper, white body, pink hair, green stripe, green/blue turtle float, pink snail shell
Wavy, purple body, orange hair, pink stripe, pink/green frog float, white spiral shell
Sea Spray, pink body, white hair, yellow stripe, green/blue lobster float, purple star shell
Surfy, yellow body, pink hair, purple stripe, blue/purple alligator float, green conch shell
Salty, blue body, purple hair, white stripe, yellow/red-orange lobster float, pink horizontal shell

Soft Sleepy Newborns

These are about 10 inch tall baby ponies. They aren't that soft really. They are made out of hard plastic and have silky hair manes & tails. They came with bonnets, panties, and pacifiers. When you pull their tail ther eyes blink. M=$50, GR=$40, G=$30, P=$15

Pink Dreams, pink body, blue hair, duck pull toy

Hushabye, white body, pink hair, blue teddy bear. *Courtesy of Stephanie Stair*

Sweet Dreams, light purple body, pink hair, pink/white bottle

Sparkle Baby Ponies

They have glittery see-through bodies. M=$5, GR=$4, G=$3, P=$2

Gusty, unicorn, yellow body, pink hair, green/pink hot air balloon
Starflower, pink body, yellow hair, green/purple stars around a center star
Firefly, pegasus, purple body, orange hair, blue/orange kite
North Star, orange body, light pink hair, purple/blue planets and stars

Teeny Tiny Babies

These little ones live up to their name. They are 2 1/2 inches tall. Very tiny and so cute! M=$5, GR=$4, G=$3, P=$2

Little Giggles, gray body, blue hair, purple A B C blocks
Little Tabby, pink body, green hair, purple bear with hat
Little Whiskers, white body, pink hair, blue rattle
Little Honey Pie, blue body, purple hair, pink bottle

10th Anniversary Babies

Came out in 1991 with the Anniversary Adults to celebrate the 10th Anniversary of pony making!

Fancy Mermaid Ponies. Pearly finish, have heart on their chest with a design in it. M=$15, GR=$12, G=$10, P=$5

Baby Pearly, pink body, pink hair, blue whale on heart
Baby Sea Princess, blue body, purple hair, pink crab on center heart
Baby Shimmer, purple body, blue hair, pink starfish on center heart

Paradise Baby. Very neon colored!
M=$15, GR=$12, G=$10, P=$5
 Baby Palm Tree, pegasus, pink body,
  neon yellow/blue hair, palm trees
 Baby Pinapple, yellow body, blue/pink
  hair, pink pineapples
 Baby Beach Ball, unicorn, orange body,
  pink/purple hair, beach ball and
  umbrella

Teeny Pony Twins. These little ones are
the cutest! M=$15, GR=$12, G=$10,
P=$5
 Sniffles & Snookums - came with a
  divided bowl and two spoons.
  Sniffles, pink body, white hair,
  sunflower w/leaves in pot, purple
  blossom on hind foot. Snookums,
  pink body, white hair, sunflower in
  flower pot, purple blossom on cheek
 Bootsie & Tootsie - came with pink &
  blue bottles. Bootsie, light purple
  body, yellow hair, yellow/blue lace
  booties, lace bootie on cheek.
  Tootsie, light purple body, yellow hair,
  yellow/blue booties, bootie on right
  front foot.
 Rattles & Tattles - came with a yellow
  and a purple baby necklace. Rattles, blue body, deep melon hair,
 purple rattle, purple bow right hind foot, *Courtesy of Stephanie
 Stair*. Tattles, blue body, deep melon hair, purple rattle, purple
 bow on forehead

Twice as Fancy Babies
 Mail Order Only! Very Rare! M= $35, GR=$30, G=$20, P=$10

Baby Up Up and Away, unicorn,
 pink body, light pink hair,
 yellow and green balloons
Baby Milky Way, pegasus, pink
 body, white hair mane has
 blue stripe, silver stars
Baby Love Melody, purple body,
 pink hair, pink hearts on a
 string
Baby Sugarberry, white body,
 deep melon hair, red
 strawberries on a vine
Baby Sweet Tooth, unicorn,
 blue body, pink hair, pink &
 blue lollipops
Baby Dancing Butterflies,
 pegasus, yellow body, yellow
 hair, butterflies

Valentines Day Sisters

Mail order only, available exclusively through Current Co. around 1988. They *did not* come with names, so I named them! M=$10, GR=$8, G=$6, P=$4

Kisses, purple baby, pink hair, pink heart with purple arrow through it
Hugs, white baby, hot pink hair, red heart with pink & red rainbow over it.

Watercolor Baby Sea Ponies

Their thread-like hair changes color in warm water. If they have their float add $2 to value. M=$5, GR=$4, G=$3, P=$2

Seashore, yellow body, white hair, orange/blue fish float
Seawinkle, purple body, green hair, pink/green alligator float
Foamy, yellow body, purple hair, blue/yellow frog float
Wavedancer, blue body, purple hair, yellow/lavender lobster float
Misty, orange body, yellow hair, purple/orange duck float
Sealight, purple body, yellow hair, green/pink turtle float

Adult and Baby Sets

There were several sets made that mixed babies and adults. All pictures read left to right and front to back. Ponies are valued at these conditions unless otherwise noted:
Mint Condition (M) no hair trims or permanent marks
Great Condition (GR) a couple minor unnoticeable marks, tiny hair snip
Good Condition (G) permanent marks, hair trims, not to bad

Poor (P) really bad off, many marks, hair cut.

Loving Family Ponies

Three different sets of Loving Families were made. Each family consists of a mommy, a daddy and a baby! They are moderately hard to find. Set: M=$35, GR=$30, G=$20, P=$15. Each: M=$10, GR=$8, G=$6, P=$4

Apple Delight Family
Daddy Apple Delight, white body, yellow hair, trees and yellow dots all over
Baby Apple Delight, white body, yellow & pink hair, pink apples and trees with apples on them
Mommy Apple Delight, white body, pink hair, pink apples and dots all over

Bright Bouquet Family
Mommy Bright Bouquet, purple body, purple hair, blue flowers all over
Baby Bright Bouquet, purple body, blue & purple hair, blue flowers and blue & purple hearts
Daddy Bright Bouquet, purple body, blue hair, blue & purple hearts all over

Sweet Celebrations Family
    Mommy Sweet Celebrations, blue body, pink hair, pink balloons all over
    Baby Sweet Celebrations, blue body, pink & green hair, green presents &
       pink balloons - boy baby
    Daddy Sweet Celebrations, blue body, green hair, green presents all over

Mommy and Baby Set
    This mail order set came with yellow crib, bottle for Baby Beachy Keen (add $2 for crib or bottle). Very rare, only one other duplicate seen. Set: M=$70, GR=$60, G=$45, P=$30

Mother Love, purple body, pink hair, mom cat and baby cat. M= $35,
    GR=$30, G=$20, P=$15
Beachy Keen, purple body, pink hair, white painted on underwear/hearts and
    baby cat - Fancy Pants. M= $30, GR=$25, G=$20, P=$15

Party Pack Ponies

See "Gift Packs & Sets" for values for the whole set with accessories. M=$6, GR=$5, G=$4, P=$2

Best Wishes, pegasus, pink body, yellow hair, blue & white candles - So Soft

Yum Yum, purple body, green hair, pink candies - Flutter Pony

Celebrate, white body, purple hair, purple/orange turtle float - Pretty 'n Pearly baby sea pony

Party Time, orange body, white/yellow/blue hair, party hats - Twinkle Eye

Frosting, unicorn, green body, white hair, yellow party hats - Beddy-Bye-Eyed baby

Play Set Ponies

This set of five ponies was available only by mail order. However they are still very easy to find. M=$4, GR=$3, G=$2, P=$1

Sprinkles, pegasus, pink body, blue hair, blue ducks - Regular Pegasus

Baby Tiddly-Winks, pink body, pink hair, white bib (no freckles) - Regular Baby Earthling

Baby Half Note, light purple body, blue hair, purple ballet slippers (no freckles) - Regular Baby Earthling

Majesty, unicorn, white body, blue hair, blue sparkly blossoms - Regular Unicorn

Lemon Drop, yellow body, purple hair, purple rain drops (writing in all four feet) - Regular Earthling

Ponies with Places

These are ponies that came with a pony place. The place is in parentheses and its type is listed after it. M=$8, GR=$6, G=$4, P=$2

Majesty, unicorn, white body, blue hair, blue sparkly blossoms (Dream Castle) - Regular Unicorn

Peachy, peach body, pink hair, pink hearts (Pretty Parlor) - Regular Earthling

Sprinkles, pegasus, lavender body, blue hair, blue ducks (Waterfall) - Regular Pegasus

Fifi, white body, blue hair, pink bows all over (Perm Shoppe) - Twice as Fancy

Scoops, white body, purple hair, soda floats all over (Satin Slipper Sweet Shoppe) - Twice as Fancy

Lemon Drop, yellow body, purple hair, purple drops (Show Stable) - Regular Earthling

Baby Half Note, purple body, blue hair, ballet slippers (Baby Bonnet School
   of Dance) - Beddy-Bye-Eyed
Baby Tiddly Winks, light purple body, pink hair, white bib (Lullabye Nursery)
   - Beddy-Bye-Eyed
Baby Half-Note, purple body, blue hair, ballet slippers, has freckles (School
   of Dance) - Regular Earthling
Baby Tiddly Winks, pink body, pink hair, white bib, has freckles (Lullabye
   Nursery) - Regular Earthling

Slumber Party Pack Ponies
See "Gift Packs & Sets" for values of the whole set. M=$6, GR=$5, G=$4, P=$2

Baby Night Cap, yellow body, pink hair, night caps - First Tooth Baby
Sleepy Head, light blue body, pink hair, pink & blue striped pajamas
Pink Dreams, light green body, pink hair, pink cat - Flutter Pony
Sleep Tight, pink body, blue hair, yellow rocking crib
Pillow Talk, grayish body, yellow/blue/white hair, white pillows/yellow moons
   all over - Twice as Fancy

Hasbro made little solid plastic ponies called Petite Ponies. They stand about 1 3/4 inches tall with horse-shoe imprints in the bottom of their little round type base. Don't worry, if you find one you will know it. They didn't have names so you will have to give them one! I will give their descriptions in the following order, body color, hair color, and design. However, the design is only on one side of their rump. All sets except for the three Pony Tail Petites have molded plastic hair.

The bottom of every Petite Pony's pedestal has a recessed horseshoe.

Pony Tail Ponies.

These ponies came in three different sets of four and have real hair tails. Each set came with a star pick. M=$3, G=$2, P=$1

1st Set. Came with orange star pick
 Pink body, pegasus, hot pink hair, orange pizza slices
 Blue body, yellow hair, purple mirror
 White body, pink hair, green brush & comb
 Yellow/orange body, purple hair, blue alarm clock

2nd Set. This set came with a red star pick. The designs are the same, but they are different colors.
 Blue body, hot pink hair, orange alarm clock
 Pink body, blue hair, purple brush & comb
 Yellow body, pegasus, blue hair, red pizza slices
 Purple body, yellow hair, orange mirror
3rd Set. *Not shown*
 Blue body, pink hair, yellow brush/comb
 Orange body, aqua hair, purple pizza slices
 Yellow body, white hair, red mirror
 Dark Pink body, yellow hair, blue alarm clock

Pretty 'n Pearly.
These have a pearly finish. A set of five was made.
M=$3, G=$2, P=$1
Orange body, purple hair, blue seashell
Yellow body, purple hair, blue feather
Purple body, pink hair, pink umbrella
Blue body, yellow hair, purple moon with night cap
Pink body, light blue hair, blue heart with wings

Pretty Pony Parade.
A set of 10 was made. M=$3, G=$2, P=$1
Yellow body, blue hair, orange sun
Purple body, green hair, white beachball
Blue body, pink hair, purple teddy bear
Green, pegasus, yellow hair, pink crayon
Pink body, yellow hair, green butterfly
Blue body, yellow hair, purple umbrella
Orange body, purple hair, blue teapot
Red body, yellow hair, white duck
Light purple body, orange hair, purple ballet slippers
White body, pegasus, pink hair, purple ice cream cone

Sun Sparkle Ponies.
These ponies came in set of five.
M=$3, G=$2, P=$1
Purple body, hot pink hair, yellow perfume bottle
Blue body, pink/purple hair, purple soda
Green body, pegasus, orange hair, purple balloons
Orange body, lavender hair, pink hot air balloon
Pink body, yellow hair, orange ring

Petite Pony Places

There were different places made for the petite ponies!

Carousel. A merry-go-round that Petite Ponies could ride. Also came with ticket booth, seesaw, a train with a teapot engine and 3 cups, fencing, slide, and two ponies. Pink body, blue hair, white pinwheel. Green body, pink hair, purple tickets. M=$12, G=$8, P=$5

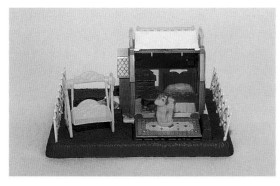

Houses. M=$8, G=$5, P=$3
   Whinny Winks Inn, pink house, white roof. Came with fencing, swing, bed, chest of drawers, table, and pony. Orange body, pink hair, blue candle.
   Not shown: Happy Hearts Cottage, yellow house, blue roof. Came with fencing, bath tub, vanity, loveseat, seesaw, and pony. Purple body, blue hair, blue duck.
   Not shown: Pony Prints Cabin, white house, pink roof. Came with fencing, couch, wishing well, bed, and pony. Pink body, blue hair, orange fish jumping out of a bowl.

Castle. Has a manual elevator in it. When the pony reaches top floor a light comes on. Came with fencing, bed, vanity, chair, dinner table, swan carriage, and 2 Pony Tail Ponies. White body, yellow hair, purple crown. Orange body, purple hair, purple wand. M=$12, G=$8, P=$5

Shoppes. M=$8, G=$5, P=$3
   Mane Delights Beauty Shoppe, purple/pink shoppe, and sign. Came with fencing, hair dryers, sink, jewelry case, coffee table, magazine stand, mirror, and Pony Tail Pony. Yellow body, pink hair, purple perfume bottle.
   Not shown: Happy Hoof Market, pink shoppe, and sign. Came with fencing, shopping cart, grocery store items, car, and Pony Tail Pony. Purple body, purple hair, ??
   Not shown: Twinkle Treat Ice Cream Shoppe, blue shoppe, and sign. Came with fencing, jukebox, booth, slide, ice cream truck, sign, and Pony Tail Pony. Green body, pegasus, yellow hair, orange (ice cream scoop)?

Animal Families

All Moms are flocked and come with two babies.

Happy Hopper & baby, Dalmation Dots, Dreamy Siamese, Sweet Spaniel & two babies, Happy Tabby & two babies

Li'l Litters

My Little Bunny Families. All mothers have cottony tails and silky forelocks, babies are all sitting with one ear down and one back M (complete family)=$10, GR (complete, some flaws)=$8, G (mostly complete)=$6, P (only one)=$2
- Happy Hopper, mom is peach with pink forelock & purple tail - a purple and a blue baby
- Fancy Floppy, mom is yellow with white forelock & yellow tail - a pink and a green baby
- Adorable Angora, mom is pink with white forelock & pink tail - a purple and a blue baby
- Cuddly Cottontail, mom is white with pink forelock & blue tail - a blue and a yellow baby

My Little Kitty Families. All mothers have cottony tails M (complete family)=$10, GR (complete, some flaws)=$8, G (mostly complete)=$6, P (only one)=$2
- Cutie Calico, blue mom with blue tail - two little blue kittens, one is asleep the other playing
- Happy Tabby, white mom w/purple stripes and white tail - sitting kitten purple/white stripes, sleeping kitten white with purple stripes
- Dreamy Siamese, pink mom/gray paws and pink tail - playing and sleeping kittens are pink w/purple paws
- Precious Persian, mom yellow with white feet/collar and yellow tail - playing kitten gold with white collar & paws, the sitting kitten is plain white

My Little Puppy Families. All have their hair in pig tails, most have silky hair M (complete family)=$10, GR (complete, some flaws)=$8, G (mostly complete)=$6, P (only one)=$2
- Lady Labrador, mom is purple with silky purple pig tails - purple sitting puppy with collar/diamond on head, the sitting puppy is purple
- Sweet Spaniel, mom is yellow with silky yellow pig tails - yellow sitting puppy w/white collar & face, yellow walking puppy w/white paw and eye ring
- Dalmatian Dots, mom is white with blue spots and silky blue pig tails - blue spotted sitting puppies
- Pretty Poodle, mom is white with pink cottony pink pig tails and forelock - pink walking puppy, green standing puppy

Nursery Families

All moms are flocked and came with two babies. Each set came with three items.

My Little Kitty. All moms have cottony tails. M (complete family)=$10, GR (complete, some flaws)=$8, G (mostly complete)=$6, P (only one)=$2
- Perky Persians, mom is orange with white tail - sitting kitten is blue w/orange stripes, sleeping kitten is orange w/blue stripes - came with yellow playpen, yellow teddy bear, and stack toy (from bottom: yellow, blue, pink, white, orange)

Sudsy Angoras, mom is pink w/white collar/paws and purple tail - white sitting kitten, pink w/white paws playing kitten - came with a blue bath tub, yellow scrub brush, and bar of soap

Slumber Time Siamese, mom is blue w/white ears & collar - blue w/white ears & paws sitting and playing kittens - came with pink cradle, purple bottle, and pink bottle.

My Little Puppy Families. Moms have their hair in doggie tails. M (complete family)=$10, GR (complete, some flaws)=$8, G (mostly complete)=$6, P (only one)=$2

Sweet Dreams Poodles, mom is purple with white cottony pig tails/forelock - pink sitting puppy, purple standing puppy - came with blue cradle, pink bottle, and yellow bottle

Funtime Spaniels, mom is blue with silky pink pig tails - blue walking puppy, pink sitting puppy - came with pink play pen, yellow teddy bear, and stacking toy(from bottom: yellow, blue, pink, white, purple)

Scrub -a- Dub Spaniels, mom is pink with silky white pig tails - pink standing puppy, yellow sitting puppy- came with white bath tub, blue scrub brush, and bar of soap.

Gift Packs & Sets

Hasbro made several different pony Gift Packs & Sets. I have listed the pony(s) name and type that came with each place or set. This is so you can look up the pony(s) easier. These are the values for the whole Gift Pack or Set, for individual pony values look under their type that is listed.

Baby Cuddles and Baby Buggy

Baby Cuddles - Beddy-Bye-Eyed baby, came with a beautiful white buggy with purple wheels that have heart shapes cut in them. It has a pink over hanging umbrella with lace around it, purple ribbon for the top, rattle, bottle, baby necklace, pink flower pillow/lace, pink flower blanket/lace, pink dot bonnet/lace, diaper. Mail Order Only. Set: M (most everything, including a perfect pony)=$25, GR=$20, G=$15, P=$10. *See "Baby and Baby Buggy" for just baby's value.*

Party Gift Pack

This gift pack has a birthday theme. It came with a table cloth, 6 plates, 6 slices of cake, 6 candles, 6 cups, cake plate, present, 10 party favors, clip on balloon, pink ribbon, green ribbon, box of party panties, 5 party hats, Pin the Tail on the Pony game, 2 tails, 2 blind folds, party time announcement, party time postcard, 5 invitations, and the following ponies: Best Wishes-So Soft Pony, Party Time-Twinkle Eyed Pony, Yum Yum-Flutter Pony, Celebration-Pretty 'n Pearly Baby Sea Pony, Frosting-Beddy-Bye-Eyed Baby. M (with most everything, including ponies perfect)=$25, GR=$20, G=$15, P=$10. *For individual pony values see their listed category.*

Princess Baby and Buggy

Scrub-A-Dub Tub Gift Pack

Came with a green tub, clear seahorse curtain, 4 white seahorse shaped legs, pink soap rack, white bar of soap, blue star sponge, pink lace towel, comb, duck toy: duck soup, yellow shower cap, and these ponies: Spring Song-Sweetheart Sister Pony, Sunny Bunch-Merry-Go-Round Pony, Sky Rocket-Sparkle Pony. M (with most everything, including perfect ponies)=$20, GR=$15, G=$10, P=$5. *For individual pony values see their listed category.*

Princess Baby Sparkle, Baby, came with a pink sparkly buggy/silvery lace, an over hanging umbrella, pink ribbon for top, pink blanket, sippy cup/lid, dish/spoon, comet hair clip, silvery hair ribbon. Set: M (with most everything, including the pony perfect)=$25, GR=$20, G=$15, P=$10, *See Baby and Baby Buggy for just baby's value.*

Slumber Party Gift Pack

Of course it has that sleep over theme. It came with a rainbow hop game, rainbow hop spinner, record player, record with case, telephone, popcorn bucket, sleeping bag, 5 night caps, hair comb, two boxes of party panties, television, box of cookies, 2 pony magazines, carton of milk, and the following ponies: Pillow Talk-Twice as Fancy Pony, Pink Dreams-Flutter Pony, Night Cap-First Tooth Baby, Sleep Tight & Sleepy Head-Newborn Twins. M (with most everything, including perfect ponies)=$25, GR=$20, G=$15, P=$10. *For individual pony values see their listed category.*

PONY PLACES & ACCESSORIES

Pony places are large hard plastic playsets for your ponies to play in. They spend most of their time in these places, eating, playing, dancing, and other sorts of things. Also accessories like cribs or carrying cases were created for the ponies.

Big green bonnet, with pink bow on top to carry it by. It opens up to reveal a dance studio. The three places on the floor turn when the wheel on the side is turned. Three different versions were made: **1st** Came with Baby Half-note, lavender body, blue hair, purple ballet slippers - Beddy-Bye-Eyed, 4 leg warmers, tutu, head piece, ballet case, 2 swan friends, 2 bee friends, 2 rabbit friends, announcement stand, 6 announcements, practice bar; **2nd** came with all the same items, but with non-Beddy-Bye-Eyed half-note (she has freckles); and **3rd** was available through mail order only and had these accessories: ballet case, 2 swan friends, 2 bee friends, 2 rabbit friends, announcement stand, 6 announcements, practice bar. For pony's individual value see "Ponies and Places" under "Adult and Baby Sets." M (with everything)=$35, GR=$30, G=$25, P=$15b

Baby Bonnet School of Dance

Brush Me Beautiful Boutique

A small purple place like a stall, came with 1 white saddle, 1 white bridle/ reins, basket and strap, yellow ribbon, pink ribbon, blanket, summer hat, flowered hat, brush, comb, Catnip - the cat, white with green stripes. M (with everything)=$20, GR=$15, G=$10, P=$5

Dream Castle

For pony's individual value see *"Ponies and Places" under "Adult and Baby Sets."* Two different ones were made:

First Edition: blue tops, pink walls, white top floors, purple bottom floor, blue draw bridge, blue throne, pink throne seat cover, purple cape, blue ring stand/4 gold rings, blue treasure chest, 2 big yellow hoops, blue hat: yellow and pink ribbons, yellow basket and lift, white flags/purple stickers, blue mirror, yellow table, 2 blue (see-through) glasses, yellow and pink felt flags, yellow star brush, dragon - Spike, and Majesty (Regular Unicorn), white body, blue hair, glittery blossoms. M (with everything)=$50, GR=$45, G=$30, P=$25

Second Edition: lime green towers, light purple walls, light purple top floors, green bottom floor, 3 pink flags, 2 big purple rings, yellow mirror, purple basket and lift, purple table, 2 purple (see-through) glasses, yellow treasure chest, yellow ring stand, 4 purple rings, lime green throne, pink cloth throne seat cover, blue blanket/purple ribbon tie, pink cloth decoration, yellow hat: blue and pink ribbons, purple ribbon, yellow pick, blue brush, dragon - Spike, no ponies. M (with everything)=$50, GR=$45, G=$30, P=$25

Home Sweet Home

Is in the same mold as the show stable. It has hot pink roof with pastel yellow carrying handle and purple weathervane. The walls are white with purple floor. Sign above door reads "Home Sweet Home" then "My Little Pony" with rainbow below. Came with 3 yellow flags (with stickers), purple weathervane, white doors with yellow hinges, all yellow bed, 3 ribbons 1st, 2nd, 3rd - all yellow with sticker, 2 purple feed pans, 2 purple shelves, 3 purple trophies, yellow jumps, lavender fences, sticker decorations. M (with everything)=$50, GR=$45, G=$30, P=$25

Lullabye Nursery

Big nursery with big alphabet letters on the outside that resemble toy blocks. Has a bottle at the front where the door is and a safety pin on top to carry it by. It came with a rocking crib, mirror, swing crib, diapers, bottles, towel, powder, rattles, and chest of drawers. There were two different ones as far as I know, all the accessories stayed the same except for the year and the baby. The Nursery first came out in 1985 and was with original baby Tiddley-Winks, pink body, pink hair, white bib, and freckles. The second one came out in 1987 and came with baby Tiddley-Winks, except this time she had Beddy-Bye-Eyes. For pony's individual value see "Ponies and Places" under "Adult and Baby Sets." M (with everything)=$50, GR=$45, G=$30, P=$25

Outside view of Lullabye Nursery.

Inside view of Lullabye Nursery

84

Megan's Place

Megan's Place is a remodeled show stable. It has a white roof with blue weather vane. It has pastel lavender walls and blue floor. Sign above door reads "Megan's Place" and below "My Little Pony" with the rainbow. Came with 3 pink flags (with stickers), blue weathervane, sticker decorations, lavender doors with pink hooks, & white fences. M (with everything)=$50, GR=$45, G=$30, P=$25

Nine Baby Carrying Case

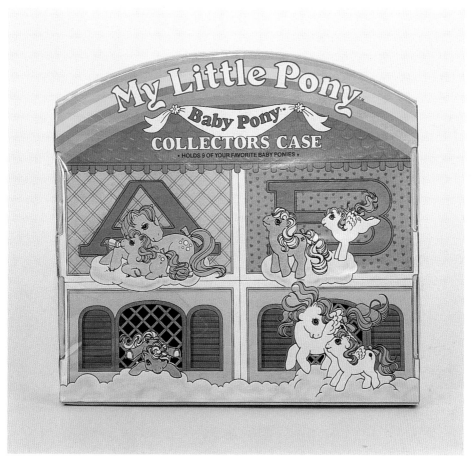

It holds 9 babies and is pictured to look like the nursery on the outside. The front is taller than rest with the rainbow and My Little Pony on it. Unusual!! VERY RARE!!! M=$35, GR=35, G=$25, P=$15

Paradise Estate

Came out in 1986. There are four large pink rooms connecting to a center patio with pool. The pool has a diving board, the patio has a table with an umbrella and two chairs, big gates open up in the front with evening lights on them. The four rooms are a kitchen, a living room, a bed room, and a nursery. The kitchen has a sink with toaster, table, chairs. The living room has a couch, easy chair, coffee table, TV, magazines. The bed room has a bed, nightstand, lamp. The nursery includes a crib, toy chest, toys, changing table. Each room has a ceiling fan and stickers to match that room.

Contents: 4 roof tops, right side of house, left side of house, patio floor, pool steps, pool lining, diving board, 4 pool canopy supports, pool canopy, 4 pool canopy inserts, left and right gate walls, left and right gates, 8 window shutters, 2 awnings with frame, 4 archways, 4 patio doors (one set for each side), 2 lanterns, 24 garden flowers, front and back pieces of two sea pony statues, bed, headboard, dresser, comb, perfume bottle, 2 lamps, living room sofa, living room chair, television, television stand, coffee table, 2 stereo speakers, sink and counter, toaster, 2 glasses, 2 milk cartons, 2 dishes, 2 forks, 2 knives, 2 spoons, breakfast bar (table), 2 stools (chairs), refrigerator, faucet, crib, crib mattress, changing table top and bottom, toy box with lid, duck pull toy, stack toy, 2 patio chairs, patio table, umbrella frame, 4 ceiling fans and posts, mylar mirror label, 3 label sheets and the instructions.

M (with everything)=$100, GR (most everything)=$60, G (all buildings and patio, pool parts, and few pieces)=$40, P (lacking buildings and major pieces)=$30. I recently found one of these MIB at an old toy store!!

Outside view

Inside view

Perm Shoppe

Big and yellow, came with Twice as Fancy Pony-Fifi. She is white, pink hair, pink bows all over. The shoppe came with rollers, roller rack, ribbons, perm spray, mirror, a stand for Fifi, cape, shower cap, ribbons, big heart mirror, vanity with heart shaped sink, and a shower that really works. M (with everything)=$50, GR=$45, G=$30, P=$25 For pony's individual value see "Ponies and Places" under "Adult and Baby Sets."

Poof 'n Puff Perfume Palace

It is shaped like a perfume bottle, and has translucent pink walls. On the top is a perfume sprayer that sprays perfume-scented air on to your pony. It came with a little vanity to hold the accessories, nail polish, lipstick, 2 necklaces, boa, 3 hair nets, 2 large barrettes, 2 small barrettes, 2 hair picks with hair, hair clip, hat, scarf, purse, brush, comb. M (with everything)=$35, GR=$30, G=$25, P=$15

Pretty Parlor

It is a small blue place that came with a purple saddle & bridle, white summer hat, yellow hat with flowers, pink brush & comb, yellow & a green ribbon, purple bridle w/ reins, purple saddle and a pink basket w/strap to carry Twinkles the cat. Twinkles is orange with black stripes. Came with the Pony Peachy (Regular Earthling), peachbody, pink hair, and pink hearts. M (with everything)=$20, GR=$15, G=$10, P=$5. *For pony's individual value see "Ponies and Places" under "Adult and Baby Sets."*

Rock-a-Bye Bed

A green bed with white cloud headboard and pink ribbon trim. Has a wheel and a picture window in headboard (different pictures appear when you turn the wheel). It came with a pink alarm clock, pink pony diary, 4 pink fuzzy slippers, a blue/white sleeping mask, nightcap, pillow, blanket with ponies on it, 2 purple rollers, comb, and 2 side tables. M=$6, G=$4, P=$2

Satin Slipper Sweet Shoppe

It looks like a big white slipper with pink bow on top for carrying it. Came with ice cream cone counter, 3 ice cream sodas, 3 ice cream sundaes, table, 2 chairs, "Today's Special" sign, heart shaped lights, apron, hat, yellow stand, & Scoops, white body, purple hair, milkshakes all over. M (with everything)=$50, GR=$45, G=$30, P=$25. *For pony's individual value see "Ponies and Places" under "Adult and Baby Sets."*

Scrub-A-Tub

The tub from the gift set was also sold by itself. It is green, with white seahorse feet, clear curtain with sea horses on it, faucets, drain plug, bar of soap, soap dish, and blue star sponge. M=$8, G=$2, P=$1.

Show Stable

White barn with purple roof with removable cupola with weather vane. Also has a carrying handle on top. Came with white bed, 6 pieces of fence, white triangle jump, white/yellow pole jump, 3 trophies, 3 ribbons: 1st, 2nd, and 3rd place, 2 window trays, window feed trough, 3 flags, cupola/weather vane, brown dog named Brandy, and Lemon drop, yellow body, purple hair, purple drops. M (with everything)=$50, GR=$45, G=$30, P=$25. *For pony's individual value see "Ponies and Places" under "Adult and Baby Sets."*

Six Pony Carrying Case

A vinyl carrying case that has picture of a stable on the outside. It can carry six ponies. The front snaps open and shut. M=$10, G=$8, P=$3

Sweet Dreams Crib

A white crib with a yellow bottom. It came with a blanket that has ponies on it, blue pillow/white lace trim, an attachable mobile, rattle, and a bottle. M=$15, GR=$10, P=$5

Sweet Ice Delight Cottage

Makes real snow cones. The ice cottage came with, table/umbrella and chairs, ice buckets, and shovel spoons. This place is really neat, I am always in search of one! M (with everything)=$50, GR=$40, G=$30, P=$15

Twelve Pony Carrying Case

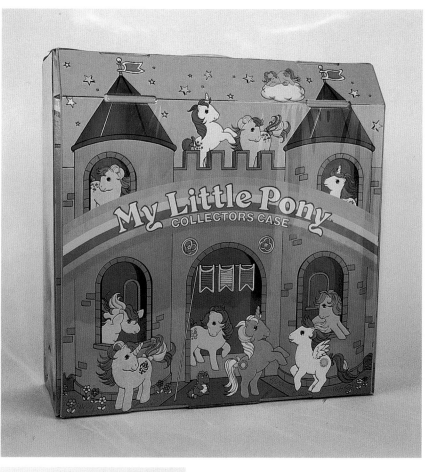

This case is about 15x15 and holds 12 ponies, The design that runs around the case is a castle with ponies playing. It has a yellow handle and has space for accessories in the bottom. Very Rare! M=$35, GR=$35, G=$25, P=$15

Waterfall

Clouds and a rainbow, with a big cloud at the bottom to hold water. Place a pony in the cloud tub and a smaller cloud at the top sprinkles the pony with water. This came with the pony Sprinkles, pegasus, lavender body, blue hair, blue ducks, duck soup the duck, and bubble bath. M (with everything)=$50, GR=$45, G=$30, P=$25. *For pony's individual value see "Ponies and Places" under "Adult and Baby Sets."*

This section will cover, you guessed it, clothes! Yes, I said clothes! There were outfits of all sorts and sizes made for adult and baby ponies, and Megan! This is definitely not all of the outfits ever made, but it is a good portion. There is probably more out there some where! A quick note on shoes: There were three different types of shoes made, plain no bows, with bows, and tennis shoes. Tennis shoes have bows on them, but also have an imprint to make them look like they are laced. Outfits are valued based on contents: M - all pieces mint, GR - most pieces, G - few pieces, P - one piece.

Lots of loose shoes are found so here is normal shoe values: a single shoe good condition = .50, set of 4 shoes mint condition = $3.

Pony-Naut

Hearts and Candy

Great Skates

Snow Angels

Sweet Dreams

Baby Pony Wear

Each outfit came with a little pocket pal to put in the pocket of the outfit. One set consists of two outfits. M=$15, GR=$10, G=$5, P=$3

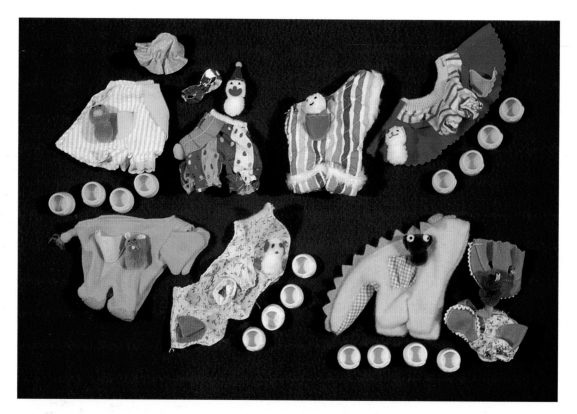

Elephant Suit-mouse pocket pal, elephant suit; Party Dress-puppy pocket pal, dress, 4 pink bow shoes
Bathrobe-duck pocket pal, bathrobe, shower cap; Clown Suit-clown pocket pal, clown suit, clown mask, 4 yellow bow shoes
Dragon Suit-dragon pocket pal, dragon suit; Sunsuit-frog pocket pal, bonnet, sunsuit, 4 white bow shoes
Jumper-kitten pocket pal, jumper, 4 yellow shoes; Snow Suit-snowman pocket pal, snow suit
Not shown: Bunny Suit-bunny pocket pal, bunny suit; Overalls-rag doll pocket pal, overalls, cap, 4 yellow bow shoes
Not shown: Lion Suit-kitty pocket pal, lion suit; Sleeper-teddy bear pocket pal, night gown, night cap, 4 green slippers

Costume Wear

M=$15, GR=$10, G=$5, P=$3

Pony-Naut, silver/gold astronaut suit & back pack, clear helmet, 4 silver glitter bow shoes

Academy Award, silver/blue/magenta dress, blue/magenta head piece, 4 magenta bow shoes

Not shown: Rockin' The Night Away, purple/silver/tie died shirt, blue pants, gold/silver guitar, silver headband, 2 tie dyed shoes, 2 magenta bow shoes

Not shown: Abra-Ca-Dabra, blue/gold genie shirt & pants, blue/ gold veil, blue/ gold hair band, 4 gold genie slippers

Not shown: Galaxy Glamour, gold/silver coat, silver pants, gold/silver rocket pack with belt, silver headband, 4 silver glitter bow shoes

Not shown: In The Center Ring, gold/silver body suit & cape, gold headdress with purple/magenta feathers, gold mask, 4 magenta bow shoes

Megan & Pony Wear

Clothes for Megan and Sundance! One set consists of two outfits. M=$15, GR=$10, G=$5, P=$3

Picnic In The Park. Megan: blue jean dress with white heart print sleeves, 2 red heart shoes, ribbon. Pony: blue jean/white heart print trim dress, 4 hard red bow shoes.

Sweet Dreams. Megan: white pale lavender flower bud nightgown, 2 lavender heart shoes, ribbon. Pony: white, pale lavender flower bud nightgown, 4 pale lavender bow shoes.

Flower Darlings. Megan: pale blue satin dress with flower print along bottom and white lace trimmed, white flower head band, ribbon, 2 white heart shoes. Pony: pale blue satin dress with flower print, 4 white bow shoes.

By The Sea. Megan: pink - purple/blue trimmed hooded jacket, blue - purple/ pink trimmed swimsuit, ribbon and clear purple sunglasses. Pony: blue - purple/pink trimmed hooded jacket.

Not shown: Country Jamboree. Megan: blue overalls, white/pink striped shirt, 2 pink shoes, ribbon. Pony: blue with pink heart and white/pink laced outfit, 4 pink bow shoes.

Not shown: Ice Princesses. Megan: pink/white fur trimmed hooded jacket, 2 pink ice skates, purple stretch pants, ribbon. Pony: pink fur trimmed hooded jacket.

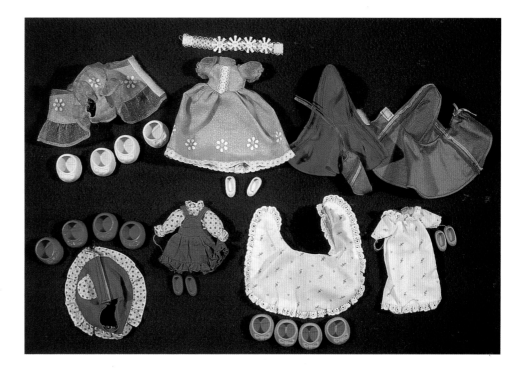

Mother/Baby Pony Wear

Each outfit has a complete set of items for the mommy and a complete set of items for the baby. These are mother and baby matching outfits. One outfit actually consists of two sets. M=$15, GR=$10, G (each piece)=$5, P=$3

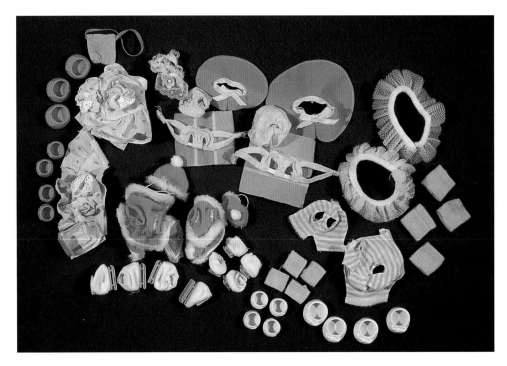

Sunday Stroll, each set consists of a pink dress with pink flower buds/white lace trim, white lace flower bonnet, pink purse, and 4 pink bow shoes (missing adult bonnet & shoe).

Snow Angels, each outfit consists of 4 white ice skates, pink/white fur trim skating dress, and pink/white fur trimmed hat.

Sun & Fun, each set consists of a pink/purple/orange/yellow beach towel, yellow/white dot bikini and pink/yellow sun hat.

Prima Ballerinas, each set consists of 4 pink fuzzy leg warmers, 4 white bow shoes, white mesh tutu, and pink/white striped leotard.

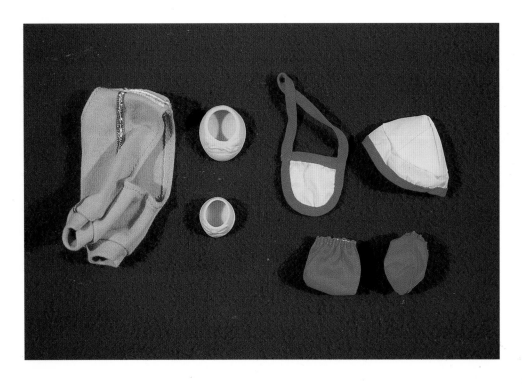

Pony Workout, each set consists of 4 orange bow sneakers, blue sweat pants & blue sweat shirt. Also shows baby shoe.

Ready for Rainbows, each set consists of a red/yellow rain coat, rain hat, 4 nylon rain boots, and a purse.

Play 'N Wear
M=$15, GR=$10, G (each piece)=$5, P=$3

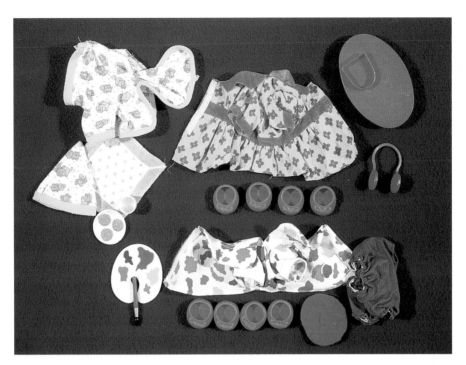

Pretty As A Picture, paint splattered smock, blue pants, red beret, red plastic brush , white plastic palette with paint, 4 soft red bow shoes

Milk 'n Cookies, white animal print night cap & night shirt with yellow trim, pink heart blanket/pink trim & pillow, white plastic cup, white plate with 3 orange cookies (missing pillow)

Pony Holiday, yellow magenta flowered dress with magenta trim, yellow sun hat with magenta ribbon, yellow suitcase, 4 magenta bow shoes (missing suitcase)

Sidewalk Surfer, orange dress with gold belt, gold visor, red headphones, 2 gold knee pads, red skateboard (skateboard and headphones shown)

Not shown: Hit The Slopes, sliver ski hat, magenta ski suit, 2 purple skis, silver goggles

Not shown: Get Into The Groove, blue/yellow trim top and yellow/blue confetti skirt (all one dress), blue socks, yellow/ blue confetti hair piece, green boom box, 4 yellow bow shoes

Pony Pack
Accessory sets for the ponies. M=$8, GR=$6, G=$5, P=$4

Accessory Set 1) 4 pink cloth leg warmers, pink plastic tennis racquet, white visor, 4 white bow shoes, white ribbon, butterfly brush

Accessory Set 2) Blue jeweled ring, blue tiara with jeweled ends, pink cloth purse, 4 purple bow shoes, purple ribbon, star comb

Not shown: Accessory Set 3) Pink shoulder bag, pink winter hat with white fur trim, white pearl necklace, 4 yellow bow shoes, pink ribbon, whale brush

Not shown: Accessory Set 4) Jeweled tiara, silver purse, pink jeweled earrings, 4 pink bow shoes, blue ribbon, bird brush

Pony Wear Set One

Original set of six "Pony Wear" outfits made. M=$15, GR=$10, G(each piece)=$5, P=$3

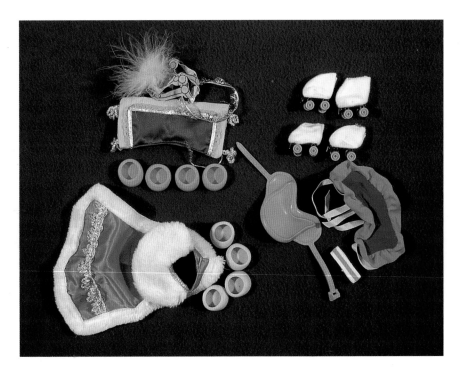

Pony Royal, pink cape with white fur trim, white crown with pink ties, 4 white shoes (cape and shoes shown)

Parade Pizzazz, pink/neon green feathered bridle, purple/pink neon green saddle pad, 4 pink shoes

Great Skates, pink english saddle, pink/purple pad w/ties, a white/pink striped sweat band, four white roller skates, pink shooting star brush, and pink ribbon

Sweet Dreams, pink cloth gown with lace trim, three purple rollers, a flower bonnet with pink ties, 4 pink fuzzy slippers

Best of the West, silver bridle with sequins and reins, pink western saddle, silver saddle blanket, 4 pink shoes (missing bridle)

The Tea Party, silky flowered party shaw with purple ties. straw hat with purple flower and pink ribbon tie, 4 pink shoes

Pony Wear Set Two

The second set of 8 outfits were made. Early on each outfit came with a scented sticker. M=$15, GR=$10, G(each piece)=$5, P=$3

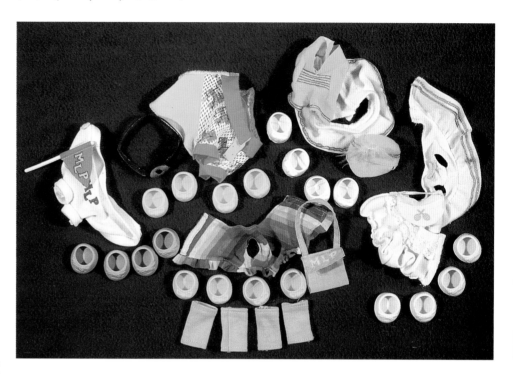

Pom Pom Pony, white cheerleader MLP sweater, pink/purple skirt, pink "MLP" pennant, pink/purple pom poms, 4 purple tennis shoes (sweater, shirt, and pennant shown)

Flash Prance, rainbow striped dress, purple MLP bag, pink headband, 4 pink leg warmers, 4 yellow bow shoes

Pony Luv, white with pink/blue trim tennis dress, white cloth shorts, 4 white tennis shoes, pink racket, white visor (missing racket)

Neon Lights, neon orange/yellow dress, with fishnet top, black belt, 4 yellow bow shoes

Strike Up The Band, white band skirt with glittery trim, yellow band jacket with glittery trim, yellow plumed hat with glittery trim, white baton, 4 hard white bow shoes (missing baton)

Not shown: Having A Luau, grass hula skirt, tropical print shirt, white hat with flower on hat band, purple purse, 4 white bow shoes

Not shown: Party Time, purple dress/white dots, party hat, birthday present, 4 pink bow shoes, pink ribbon

Not shown: City Kids, yellow blouse with blue skirt, pink purse, purple belt, 4 yellow bow shoes and four pink cloth slippers

Pony Wear with Jewelry

Each came with a piece of costume jewelry for the pony to wear. M=$15, GR=$10, G (each piece)=$5, P=$3

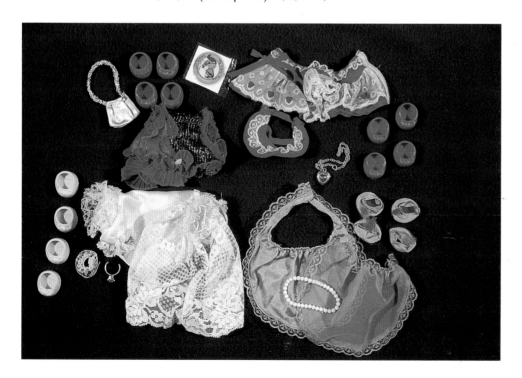

Something Old - Something New, white satin dress, white veil with silver crown, silver diamond ring, 4 bow shoes

Sweetness and Lace, purple silk nightgown, purple silk robe, white pearl necklace, 4 soft purple feathered slippers

From The Designer Collection, magenta and black dress, silver purse, jeweled earrings, 4 magenta bow shoes (missing earrings)

Hearts and Candy, red/ white lace valentine dress, red/white laced hat, silver heart pendent on pink chain, 4 hard red bow shoes

Not shown: Pageant Queen, silver gown, purple "Miss Pony USA" ribbon, silver purse, silver crown, 4 purple bow shoes

Not shown: Lights, Camera, Action, gold gown trimmed with white fur, gold sunglasses, 4 blue bow shoes

Pretty Ups

ILY stands for "I Luv You" hair barrettes that came with each set. There are also two "hair combs" in each set. M=$15, GR=$10, G(each piece)=$5, P=$3

Kittens and Teddies: Blue hair clip with purple hair; 1 pink & 1 green bear barrette; purple dog comb with pink hair braid and 1 green & 1 pink bead; small yellow dog comb with aqua hair and blue bead; 1 yellow and 1 blue small dog barrettes; pink ribbon; pink duck comb

Seashore: 1 green & 1 blue fish barrette; blue shell comb with blue hair braid and 1 purple & 1 lavender bead; small coral shell with yellow hair/pink strands and a yellow bead; 1 pink and 1 yellow small starfish barrette; green hair clip with pink hair; yellow ribbon; green fish comb

Ribbons and Lace: aqua bow comb with yellow hair braid and 1pink & 1yellow bead; 1 purple & 1 green small barrette; 1 blue & 1 pink large ILY barrettes; small red bow comb with white/gold strands and white bead; purple hair clip with aqua hair; blue ribbon; lavender bird brush.

Birds and Flowers: white flower comb with pink hair braid and 1 pink & 1 green bead; small blue bird comb with yellow/colored strands and yellow bead, 1 green & 1 blue small flower barrette, 1 yellow & 1 lavender large barrette, purple hair clip with pink hair, sea green ribbon, and blue butterfly brush.

Hasbro made many different items with ponies on them. Here are the ones I know of to date.

Accessory Set

A purple snap shut box 6 x 5 x 1.5 inches, a purple change purse, a purple wallet with mirror and pony picture, and a pony picture in a purple frame. This set is made of plastic type stuff. M (with everything)=$15, GR=$10, G (just one item)=$5, P=$1.

Address Book

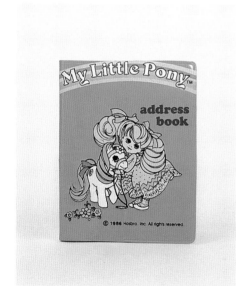

Bank

Pony coin bank, blue with pink hair (molded not real hair) and no design. Blossom, and Bow Tie have been spotted out there. M=$15, GR=$10, G=$5, P=$1 (Right)

Bed Blanket

A beautiful blanket was made for a child's bed. It features ponies playing in the clouds and has pink satin trimmed edges. M=$20, GR=$15, G=$10, P=$5 (Below)

I found a little cover dated 1986, that says address book. It is blue with a picture of Molly and baby Sundance on it with the MLP rainbow. Its dimensions are 8 1/2 cm wide by 11 cm tall. M (unwritten in)=$5, G=$3, P=$1

Bed 'n Breakfast Tray

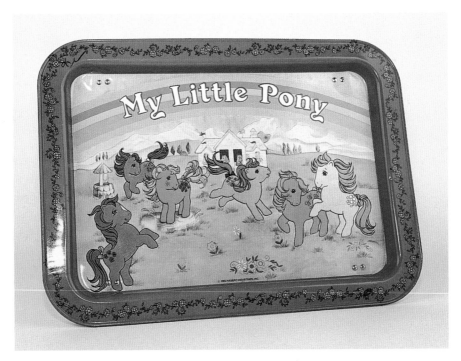

Made in 1983, it pictures ponies playing outside the stable. It is about 12 inches wide x 17 inches long, and stands a little over 6 inches from the bed, folding flat for storage. M=$15, GR=$10, G=$8, P=$5

Pillow Cases

A set of two pillow cases was also sold separately from the original sheet set. Pricing is for one pillow case: M=$6, GR=$5, G=$3, P=$1

Bed Set

Not shown: This set consists of a fitted bottom sheet, top sheet, and 2 pillow cases. They have the beautiful print of ponies playing in the clouds on them. They came mostly in twin and full, but I have seen queen size. M (set)=$35, GR (worn)=$30, G (missing pieces)=$20, P (each)=$10.

Curtains

Not shown: A set of curtains, featuring ponies playing in clouds. They were made to go with the bedding so you could decorate your own pony room. M=$35, GR=$25, G=$15, P $10

Duffel Bag

Not shown: Light blue with pink handles and trim, pictures Megan and Sundance on it. M=$25, GR=$20, G=$15, P=$5

Bubble Bath

Pony-shaped container that holds bubble bath . I have only found one of these so far. It looks like a merry-go-round pony. There were probably other different ones made. M=$10 (still has soap), G=$8, P=$6

Candy Container??

I found a pink and white (8.5cm tall, 3cm wide and 4.5cm wide) rectangular thing that looks like the nursery with a blue bow on top and a safety pin. On one side there is a door shaped like a bottle and hole in that side. I think maybe it held candy at one time. On the front it has a pony head with "My Little Pony" under it. On the back it has blocks that spell BABY. M=$5, G=$3, P=$1

Cake Set

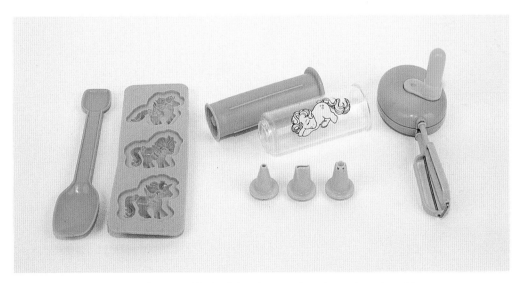

In this set there is a blue/pink hand mixer, clear decorating tube with three decorative ends and pink plunger, a mold to make three different icing ponies for decoration, a blue two ended stirring/ measuring spoon, a rolling pin, and a spatula. M (with everything)=$25, GR=$20, G=$15, P=$10

Cases

Not shown: There is a large square one, a small rectangle, and a purse type one. They are made of light blue plastic, with ponies playing in the clouds at night all over them. The measurements are as follows - Large: 13 x 10 x 3 inches, Small: 8 x 4 x 3 inches, Purse: 7 x 6 x 2 inches. Each: M=$30, GR=$25, G=$15, P=$5. I found another one about the size of the large one it and is a dark blue with a picture on the top. It pictures: Moondancer, Firefly, Applejack, Bow Tie and a couple others playing in the clouds at night.

Cassette Player

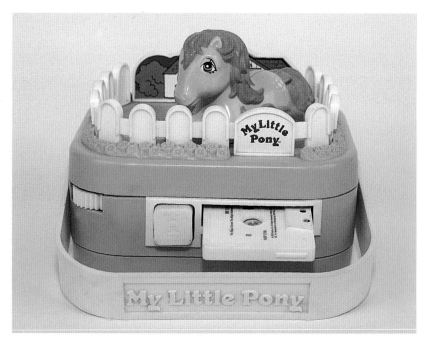

It sits on a square green base dated 1983. On top there is a white fence with "My Little Pony," and a stable background. Cotton Candy is sitting inside, and the speaker is there to. I think Hasbro made one of each of the original six ponies. Did not come with tape. M (works)=$30, GR=$25, G=$20, P=$15.

Coloring books: *Sea Ponies: My First Coloring Book; The Sea Ponies; Coloring and Activity Book;* and *In The Country*

Coloring Books

Coloring books were filled with stories and on the back cover pictured ponies and their names. These are a great source of information. Here are the ones I have. Be on the look out for more. M (not colored in)=$5, GR=$4, G=$3, P=$1

　　1984 Coloring and Activity Book
　　1984 In the Country
　　1985 The Sea Ponies
　　1986 Sea Ponies: My First Coloring Book
　　1987 Trace 'n Rub
　　1988 Show And Tell
　　1988 Magical Day
　　1988 Sweets And Treats
　　1988 All Day Long
　　1988 Ribbons And Rainbows
　　1988 All Aboard

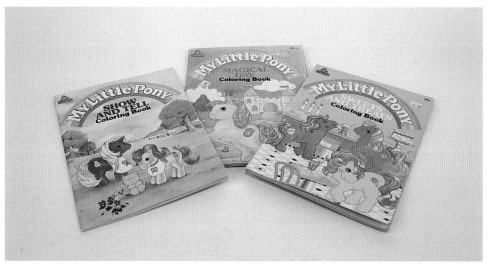

Coloring books: *Show And Tell;Magical Day;* and *Sweets And Treats*

Fan Club Member's Kit

Some of the many items included in Pony Fan Club packets throughout the years. The items are from 1987, and include a note pad, a white change purse, fan club card, and iron on decal. Price per an item: M=$5, GR=$4, G=$3, P=$2

Fashion Bag

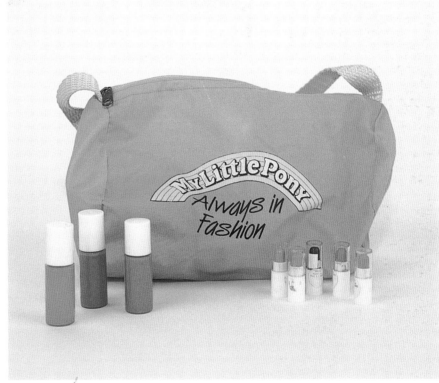

A pink fashion bag, for pony make-up, was available through the mail. It is pink canvas with pink strap. Pony make-up came in specially marked pony packages. M=$15, GR=$12, G=$8, P=$4

Fashion Make-up

Available only with ponies in specially marked pony packages. An assortment of lipstick, nail polish, and eye shadows were made. You could dress your ponies up or wear it yourself. However the make-up does fade ponies over time, so be careful. Each: M=$8, GR=$6, G=$4, P=$2

Folders

Pony folders printed with scenes from the different Pony movies.
M=$6, GR=$5, G=$4, P=$2

Games

Hasbro made 5 different games that know of.

Pony Round Up Game. A 3D stand up game that came
with: 3-D stand up game board, 3-D stand-up pieces
(stable, mountain, back drop), spinner, 18 My Little Pony
characters, 18, plastic bases, 14 My Little Pony tokens.
M(with everything)=$25, GR=$20, G=$10, P=$5

A Prize Winning Pony Race, came with: 4 pony
playing pieces, 4 pony platforms, 24 prize cards, and
1 die. M (with everything)=$15, GR=$10, G=$5,
P=$1

Carousel Pony Board Game came with: merry-go-round wheel & button, 4 pony pieces, 4 pony platforms, 28 gold rings, 12 free ride tokens, 1 die. Fairly common game. M (with everything)=$10, GR=$8, G=$6, P=$3

Merry-Go-Round Stamper Game came with: 1 merry-go-round, 16 pony cards, score pad, and 4 pony ink stamps. M (with everything)=$20, GR=$15, G=$10, P=$5

Not shown: Baby Blue Ribbon's game "Adventures in Ponyland" came with: Baby Blue Ribbon, blue ribbon prize, cardboard die, and game board. "Adventure" cards were available in pony packages to go along with the game. *See "Baby Blue Ribbon" for picture and pricing.*

Gumball Machine

Has Firefly Mom & Baby on it. You put a penny in and turn to get a gumball. M=$15, GR=$10, G=$5, P=$1

Hair Wear

Not shown: Sets include a headband, 2 barrettes, and two pony tail holders all with the same pony on them. I am not sure how many sets were made, but there is at least 6 different pony sets (Medley, Twilight are a couple). M (complete)= $8, GR=$6, G=$4, P=$1

Ironing Board

Was made for Hasbro in 1984 by Wolverine. It stands about 15 inches and is 19 1/2 inches across the top. It has The ponies Surprise and Posey in the clouds, and Firefly and Blossom on the ground. It also has a dog and a duck on it, with the My Little Pony rainbow. M=$15, GR=$12, G=$10, P=$5

Light Bright Pages

These were made by Hasbro to go on the Light Bright. Each page feautures a different pony on it to punch with specific color pegs. Once done, plug the Light Bright in and the colored pegs light up. It contains 12 pony pictures and 24 create your own sheets. M (not punched)=$10, G(some punched)=$5, P=$1

Lunch Boxes

Lunch boxes of all types were made with all kinds of different pictures on the front. M (with thermos)=$15, G=$8, P=$5

Light purple with Peek-a-Boo babies on front, all on a blanket picnicking outdoors.

Purple with Rainbow Curl ponies on front.

Blue with Candy Cane ponies on it.

Pink with Gusty and her baby, Whizzer, Sea Baby in pond, and couple of others - Megan & Sundance on thermos. These are the few I know of. Be on the look out for others.

Movies

Hasbro made several pony movies. I have three listed here, but I do think there are more out there. "Firefly's Adventure", "My Little Pony: The Movie", and "Escape from Catrina." M (with box)=$15, GR=$12, G=$10, P=$5

Mug

White plastic mug with Glory and Parasol on it, and the Pony rainbow. It stands about 4 inches high. M=$5, GR,=$4, G=$3, P=$2

Paintable Pony Statues

These guys are really neat! They are pony statues and they come with paint and brushes so could you paint them. They are made of a plaster-like substance and stand about 3 1/2 inches high. I am not sure how many were made. An unpainted statue: M=$10, GR=$8, G=$6, P=$4, a painted one $5 maximum if paint job is good.

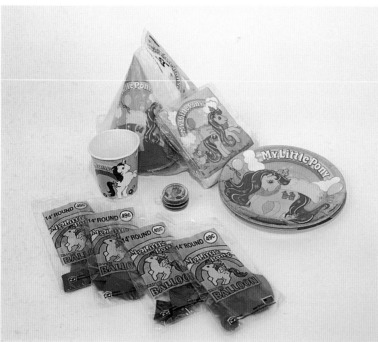

Party Items

There were all type of plates, cups, napkins and favors made with an assortment of ponies on them for birthday parties. Hasbro also made puffy name tags, and a sign-in poster. I am sure that there is more than this out there. A single item: M=$1, G=.50, P=.25

Party balloons, cup, yo-yo, party hats, napkins, & plate

Signable party poster and name tags.

Pencil By Number

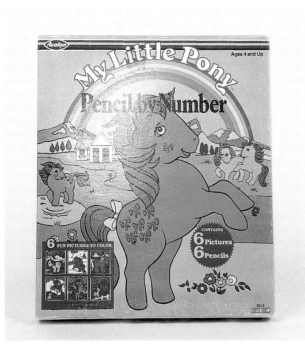

The Pencil by Number set comes with 6 colored pencils, 6 pony pictures to color, and lots of room for imagination. M (not colored)=$10, GR=$8, G=$5, P=$3

Pony Clock

Pony Clocks stand about 10 inches tall and from nose to tail are about 10 inches wide. They are 3-D with a clock in their left side. On their right side is a removable panel to easily change the battery. Also on the right side are the knobs for setting the clock . Moondancer is pictured above, but I have seen a Twilight clock. Possibly more are out there. M=$30, GR=$25, G=$20, P=$10

Pony Pendants/Pins/Apparel

Hasbro made some really cute pony pendants. I have a Blossom pendant which is pictured. M=$5, G=$3, P=$2. Hasbro also made pony pins and hair tie sets. I have a Twilight (regular unicorn) which is pictured. M=$8, G=$6, P=$4

Blossom Pony Pendant

Twilight pony pin & hair tie

Posters

These posters came in a two-pack. One picture is on cardboard and the other is on a big sheet of paper. It also came with five markers to color them with. M (not colored w/markers)=$15, GR (not colored)=$10, G=$5, P=$2

110

Puzzles

Radio

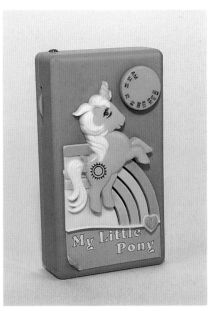

Hasbro made a variety of different pony puzzles. They come in 125 piece, 100 piece, and 24 piece. Here are the ones I have and some others I have seen. I have included dates and the edge colors of the boxes. M (all pieces)=$5, GR=$4, G=$3, P=$1

125 Pieces:
  1983 blue: Ponies on a ranch: Bow Tie, Apple Jack, & Blossom
  1985 pink: Medley and Glory in front of a castle near a lake

100 Pieces:
  1985 purple: Ponies playing in clouds, pony waterfall, water is being sprinkled
  1985 blue: Posey, Majesty, Surprise, & Heart-throb, ponies in front of Dream Castle, b-day party
  1989 purple: 4 Sweetheart Sister ponies, some ducks carrying flags, Dream Castle in the back, pond
  1990 pink: 3 PromQueens in front of a gazebo
  1989 pink: Candy Cane ponies outside of a ginger-bread house
  1987 lt. pink: 5 Twice as Fancy ponies, 2 Newborn Twins with yellow rabbits having a picnic
  1987 lt. green: 2 adults/2 Bushwoolies inside Dream Castle, 2 adults and a baby outside

24 Pieces:
  1985 green: Firefly and Baby Firefly in nursery
  1985 orange: Peachy and Baby Cuddles in buggy outside
  1987 Blue: Sugarberry looking over Newborn Twins Sniffles & Snookums in a bassinet
  1990 purple: 3 ballerina ponies dancing to music from a boom box in a studio setting
  1988, green: Windy Wing ponies playing in the ocean
  1988 blue: baby ponies and pals outside a Cinema
  1988 red: Fancy Pants and Playtime Brothers at a birthday party
  1988 green: Baby Squirmy(snail) in crib, & Baby Tappy(shoes) on floor - in nursery

Portable A.M. pony radios were made and came with headphones. I have one that pictures Sunbeam (regular unicorn) on it. Probably others were made. M=$15 (works/has head phone), GR=$10, G=$6, P=$4

Roller Skates

Pony roller skates featuring pony logos and designs were made for young girls. They came in a variety of sizes with a variety of ponies. They are just adorable. M=$20, GR=$15, G=$10, P=$5

Shrinky Dinks

You color them, cut them out, then bake them and they shrink before your eyes!! I do not know all the details, but they are really neat! Unbaked shrinky dinks: M=$5, GR=$4, G=$3, P=$2. Baked shrinky dinks about $2 to $3 dollars. *Given to me by Betsy Groff.*

Sleeping bags

I have only seen three, but I know there are more out there. M=$25, GR=$20, G=$15, P=$5

Ponies on the ground and up in the clouds with Dream Castle. Has the "My Little Pony" logo and rainbow at top. Each pony has a ribbon in its mouth, the ribbon's other end is attached to a Maypole. The ponies are dancing around the Maypole.

Not shown: Flutter ponies playing up in clouds. Paradise Estate down on land with a stream and bridge. Also has ponies playing on the ground.

Stampers

Two different kinds of pony stampers were made. The first kind was made in 1984 and they were actually shaped and colored like a pony and even stood in the pony's pose. Moondancer, Firefly, Twilight, Windy, Sky Dancer, Cotton Candy, & Bow Tie have been seen. M (with ink bottom)=$10, GR=$8, G=$6, P=$4. The second kind was made in 1985. They are small stamps with a black/white picture of the pony on the stamper. Majesty, Sunbeam, Moondancer, Glory, Butterscotch, Bluebelle, Snuzzle, and Minty have all been seen. M(with ink bottom)=$1, G=$.50, P=.25

Sticker Books

There were several sticker books made. It is a long card back and about half way down has plastic-spiral bound hard pages. It came with a sheet of puff stickers. There are several different color coded sections and you had to buy sticker packs for each section. The two I know of are "Adventure Sticker Book" in the shape of the Show Stable, and "Fantasy Sticker Book" in shape of the Dream Castle. M (with first set of stickers)=$6, G=$4, P=$2

Stickers

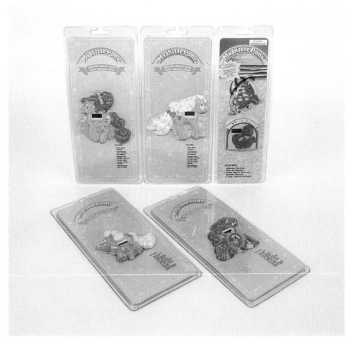

Sets of four hologram metallic stickers were made featuring different ponies. The stickers are about 4 inches by 4 inches and there are four to a package. M=$5, GR=$4, G=$3, P=$2

Stick On Clock

Two types of these were made. The first are clocks actually shaped and colored like a pony with adhesive backing made in 1990. Their sizes range from 3 x 3 inches to 4 3/4 x 3 inches. M=3, G=2, P=$1. The second kind was made in 1995 and is about 2 1/2 inches tall and 2 1/4 inches wide with adhesive backing. It is square with a curved top. It has the pony rainbow and a purple pony with pink hair and umbrella on it. M=$2, G=$1.50, P=$1

Story Books/Read Alongs

All types and sizes of story books were made. I only have a few story and read along books, but I have listed them for you.

Story books. M=$8, GR=$6, G= $4, P= $2
   1984 *New Friends*
   1984 *At The Country Fair*
   1985 *Under The Big Top*
   1985 *Mystery Chase*
   1985 *Baby Firefly's Adventure*
   1985 *Spike and the Magic Horseshoes*
   1986 *Make A Wish*
   1991 *Pretty Pony Parade*
   1991 *Dance 'n Prance*
   1991 *Sweet Dreams*

Read Along Books. M(set)=$8 , GR=$8, G(each)=$5, P= $3
   1984 *Adventure Book*/Tape
   1985 *The Magic Rainbow*/Tape
   1985 *Lost In The Clouds*/Record
   1986 *Glory The Magic Unicorn*/Tape
   Baby Blossom came with a story tape: "Listen 'n Fun" Set:
      M=$25, GR=$20, G=$15, P=$5
   Baby Ember came with a story tape: "Listen 'n Fun"-*see page 54 for picture.*

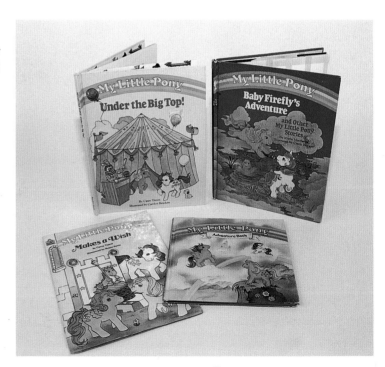

Story Books
Under The Big Top, Baby Firefly's Adventure, Makes A Wish, and *Adventure Book*

Story Books
Sweet Dreams, Pony Parade, Dance and Prance, Spike and the Magic Horseshoes, Mystery Chase, At The Country Fair, and *New Friends*

Read Along Books
Lost in the Clouds, Glory the Magic Unicorn, and *The Magic Rainbow*

Tape Case

The case holds 6 Read Along tapes and books and measures about 9 1/2 inches wide x 9 inches long x 2 inches deep. The outside pictures Dream Castle, Majesty, Moondancer, Sunbeam, Glory and the pony rainbow. It also has convenient carrying strap so you take it wherever you go. M=$25, GR=$20, G=$10, P=$5

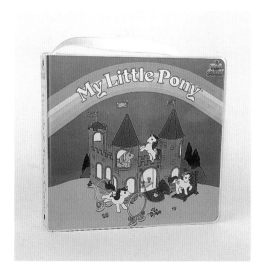

Front of tape case

Inside view of tape case

Tea Set

Without knowing what came in the original set it is hard to price it. I found a pitcher and three tea cups which possibly belonged to a 4 place setting. I do not know if there was a sugar bowl, creamer, utensils, or plates. The pitcher is about 3.5 inches tall with Bow Tie (with pink hearts, not her bow ties) and Firefly (with white spots, not her lightning bolts). The cups are about 1.5 inches tall and each have Firefly, Glory and Blossom on them (with correct designs). It was made in 1984 by Hasbro.

Tote Bag

The tote bag is purple with pink trim and inside is an attached change purse. It also has half a pony sewn on the front. It is big enough to hold books. M=$10, GR=$8, G=$6, P=$4

Vanity Set

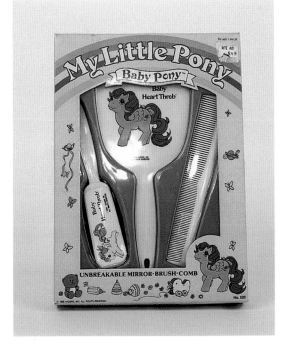

A vanity set consisting of a brush, comb, and mirror was made for a young girl to use. Each piece has a cute little baby pony on it. M=$15, GR=$10, G=$5, P=$3

Wall Decorations

They are called "Do It Yourself Room Decorations" and were produced by Priss Prints Inc. in 1990. It is a 10 pc. set of removable, and reusable mylar stick-ups. It includes jumbo ponies Dainty, Sand Digger, and Flower Bouquet, the My Little Pony Rainbow, a pair of butterflies, duck w/ flowers, duck w/net, bird w/ribbon, sun, and flowers. M=$10, GR=$8, G=$6, P=$4. *Picture Courtesy of Julie Brix*

Watches

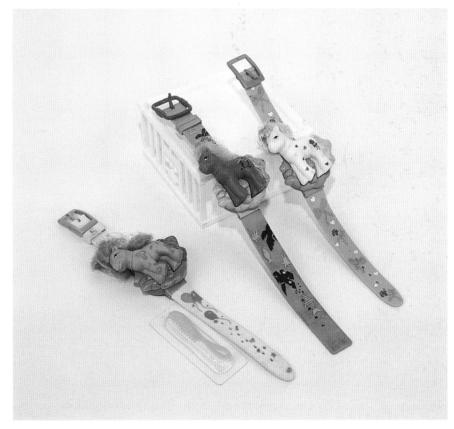

There were many different watches made, some that open, exposing the clock underneath, bracelet watches, and regular watches. M=$15, GR=$10, G=$5, P=$1.

In this section I have listed items that some adults and babies came with.

Mint In Package Ponies (Owned and Seen)

Not shown: Big Brother Chief: Blue race car comb, red fireman's hat. M=$35, GR=$30, G=$25, P=$10

Not shown: Big Brother Quarterback: Pink grasshopper comb, pink bandana, pink/purple helmet M=$35, GR=$30, G=$25, P=$10

Not shown: Big Brother Slugger: Light green grasshopper comb, pink bandana, blue baseball cap M=$35, GR=$30, G=$25, P=$10

Not shown: Big Brother Wig Wam: Orange head dress, pink grasshopper comb. M=$35, GR=$30, G=$25, P=$10

Princess Pristina (1987): Pink diamond clip on crown, dark pink wand, blue glitter star pick, pink/gold trimmed ribbon. M=$40, GR=$35, G=$30, P=$20

Princess Royal Blue (1986): Blue damsel hat/glittery silver moons & stars, pink/gold trimmed flowing ribbons. Bushwoolie Wishful: sparkly purple wand, glitter purple star pick, white/gold trimmed ribbon. M=$40, GR=$35, G=$30, P=$20

Princess Moondust (1987): Green diamond clip-on crown, pink wand, purple glitter star pick, white/gold trimmed ribbon. M=$40, GR=$35, G=$30, P=$20

Regular Pegasus Firefly: Lavender shooting star brush, white ribbon, sticker M=$25, GR=$20, G=$15, P=$10

PromQueen Sweetheart Sister Cha Cha: Bottle Perfume, pink/silver prom dress, purple flower barrette, glittery green star pick. M=$40, GR=$35, G=$30, P=$20

Showtime Dream Beauty Circle Dancer's box: pink "I Luv You" barrette, purple twisted pick

Sippin Soda Pony Strawberry Scoops: Green lollipop brush, purple/
brown/white chocolate soda. M=$40, GR=$35, G=$30, P=$20
Not shown: So Soft Taffy: Blue butterfly brush, yellow ribbon.
M=$35, GR=$30, G=$25, P=$10

Sweetberry Pony Raspberry Jam: Lavender flower brush, blue ribbon
M=$20, GR=$15, G=$10, P=$5
Not shown: Sweetberry Pony Cherry Treats: Green butterfly brush,
purple ribbon M=$20, GR=$15, G=$10, P=$5
Not shown: Twice As Fancy Pony Bonnie Bonnets: Blue butterfly brush,
blue ribbon M=$35, GR=$30, G=$25, P=$10
Not shown: Twice As Fancy Pony Dancing Butterflies: Purple sun pick,
blue ribbon M=$35, GR=$30, G=$25, P=$10
Not shown: Twice As Fancy Pony Sugarberry: Pink sun pick, yellow
ribbon M=$35, GR=$30, G=$25, P=$10

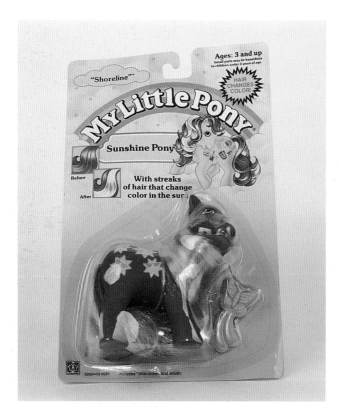

Sunshine Pony Shoreline: Green Butterfly brush M=$20, GR=$15,
G=$10, P=$5
Not shown: Sunshine Pony Sand Digger: Pink butterfly brush M=$20,
GR=$15, G=$105, P=$5
Not shown: Sunshine Pony Wavedancer: Blue sun pick M=$20,
GR=$15, G=$10, P=$5

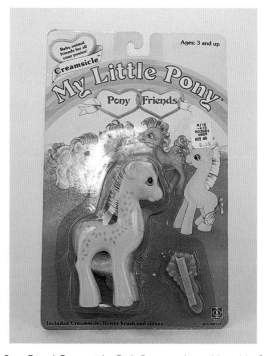

Baby Pony Friend Creamsicle: Pink flower, white ribbon M=$15,
GR=$12, G=$10, P=$5

Beddy-Bye-Eyed Baby Lickity - Split: Yellow high chair/pink tray, white bottle/pink top, blue/white divided dish & yellow spoon, yellow box of diapers, white BABY necklace, white heart bib/light blue trim, blue duck comb, white ribbon, sticker. M=$40, GR=$35, G=$30, P=$20

Beddy-Bye-Eyed Baby Shady: Lt. pink playpen, yellow pull duck(pink wheels), white heart bib/light green trim, lt. green BABY necklace, box of diapers, white bottle/yellow top, lt. green duck comb, pink ribbon, sticker: My Shady mint in package came with Scrumptious' sticker!?! M=$40, GR=$35, G=$30, P=$20

Not shown: Drink 'n Wet Baby Flicker: Green bottle, purple & green diapers, blue changing table, purple duck comb, green ribbon. M=$40, GR=$35, G=$30, P=$20

Not shown: Drink 'n Wet Baby Flicker: Purple bottle, purple & green diapers, yellow changing table, lavender duck comb, hot pink ribbon. M=$40, GR=$35, G=$30, P=$20

First Boy Baby Lucky: Purple bow tie, white moon crescent comb
M=$25, GR=$20, G=$15, P=$10

Fancy Pants Baby Glider: She is wearing a hot
pink net bow, and came withwhite sipper
cup(teddy bear in pink), duck pull toy with
pink wheels, blue dish & dark pink spoon,
green duck comb, yellow ribbon. M=$35,
GR=$30, G=$25, P=$15

First Tooth Baby Lickity-Split: Green/yellow
glow worm, pink butterfly teething ring, star
party panties, yellow tube of tooth paste/lt.
green tooth brush, lt. blue duck comb, white
ribbon. M=$35, GR=$30, G=$25, P=$15

First Tooth Baby Quackers: White tooth pillow/blue flowers(has felt tooth in it), pink tooth brush/green tube of tooth paste, stack toy from bottom: blue, yellow, lavender, pink, green), star party panties, purple duck comb, orange ribbon. M=$35, GR=$30, G=$25, P=$15

Not shown: First Tooth Baby North Star: Glow worm toy, lt. blue butterfly teething ring, star panties, blue tooth brush & tooth paste, pink duck comb, blue ribbon. M=$35, GR=$30, G=$25, P=$15

Not shown: First Tooth Baby Bouncy: xylophone toy(small to large section color: pink/blue/yellow/green/pink) with blue drum stick, blue tooth brush & pink tooth paste, sipper cup, star panties, yellow duck pull toy with pink wheels, ribbon. M=$35, GR=$30, G=$25, P=$15

Not shown: First Tooth Baby Fifi: xylophone toy(small to large section color: pink/blue/yellow/green/pink) with blue drum stick, blue tooth brush & pink tooth paste, sipper cup, purple duck comb, pink ribbon, star panties. M=$35, GR=$30, G=$25, P=$15

Not shown: First Tooth Baby Tic Tac Toe: First tooth pillow, blue tooth brush & green tooth paste, stack toy (small to large ring color) pink/blue/yellow/green/pink, star panties, pink duck comb, white ribbon. M=$35, GR=$30, G=$25, P=$15

Not shown: Newborn Twins Jangles & Tangles: Light purple & pink snail rockers, yellow dish w/ two pink spoons, 2 white flannel nightgowns with flower buds and green bows, two small white bottles, two white velcro diapers with boxes, pink & purple bear brushes, two yellow ribbons. M=$50, GR=$45, G=$40, P=$30

Not shown: Newborn Twins Milkweed & Tumbleweed: Purple bassinet with pink hood, white/blue & white/yellow rattles, purple & yellow bear brushes, two small white bottles, two white velco diapers with boxes, two purple ribbons. M=$50, GR=$45, G=$40, P=$30

Not shown: Newborn Twins Dibbles & Nibbles: Aqua bassinet with yellow hood, two rattles(colors??), two small white bottles, two white velcro diapers with boxes, two pink ribbons. M=$50, GR=$45, G=$40, P=$30

Not shown: Newborn Twins Doodles & Noodles: Light green & yellow snail rockers, yellow divided dish with two white spoons, 2 white flannel nightgowns with flower buds and pink bows, two small white bottles, two white velcro diapers with boxes, two white ribbons, yellow & purple bear brushes. M=$50, GR=$45, G=$40, P=$30

Not shown: Newborn Twins Rattles & Tattles: Dark pink stroller with light pink awning, purple & yellow bear brushes, light pink & dark pink BABY necklaces, two small white bottles, two white velcro diapers with boxes, two yellow ribbons. M=$50, GR=$45, G=$40, P=$30

Not shown: Newborn Twins Jabber & Jebber: Pink sandbox, pink & purple Baby necklaces, two small white bottles, pink & green bear brushes, two pink ribbons, two white velcro diapers and boxes. M=$50, GR=$45, G=$40, P=$30

Peek-a-Boo Baby Snippy: White butterfly bib with purple trim, green duck comb, light blue ribbon M=$15, GR=$12, G=$10, P=$5

Peek-a-Boo Baby Sweet Stuff: White butterfly bib with blue trim, yellow bear brush, yellow ribbon M=$15, GR=$12, G=$10, P=$5

Play Time Baby Brother Waddles: Pink dish/blue spoon, blue/orange xylophone with orange stick, green & white striped neckerchief, blue dog brush, pink ribbon. M=$35, GR=$30, G=$25, P=$15

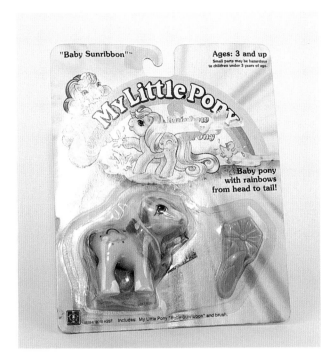

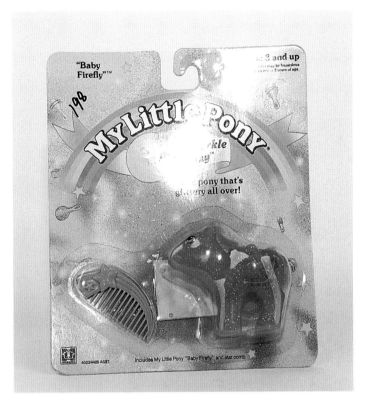

Sparkle Baby Firefly: Blue star comb M=$15, GR=$12, G=$10, P=$5

Rainbow Baby Sunribbon: Salmon flower brush M=$15, GR=$12, G=$10, P=$5

Not shown: Regular Sea Baby Sea Star: orange whale brush, yellow/purple lobster float M=$20, GR=$15, G=$10, P=$5

Not shown: Regular Sea Baby Surfrider: blue/purple fish float, yellow whale brush M=$20, GR=$15, G=$10, P=$5

Not shown: Regular Unicorn Baby Glory: Pink crib, pink ribbon, pink BABY necklace, pink bear brush, stack toy (small to large ring color) pink/white/green/yellow/blue, white with blue ring bottle, purple star blanket, diaper with box, sticker. M=$50, GR=$45, G=$40, P=$30

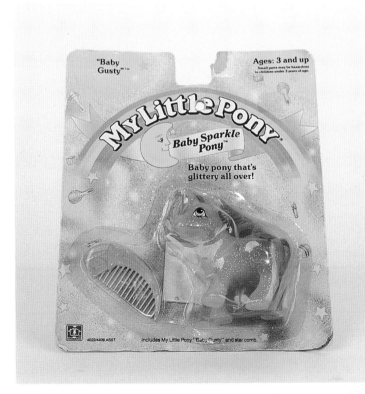

Sparkle Baby Gusty: Pink star comb M=$15, GR=$12, G=$10, P=$5

10th Anniversary Teeny Pony Twins Rattles & Tattles: Yellow baby necklace, purple baby necklace. M=$20, GR=$15, G=$10, P=$5

125

Watercolor Baby Sea Baby Sea Shore: Orange and blue fish float, blue fish comb, purple ribbon. M=$15, GR=$12, G=$10, P=$5

Watercolor Baby Sea Baby Sea Winkle: Pink and green alligator float, purple fish comb, pink ribbon M=$15, GR=$12, G=$10, P=$5

Some of the Pony's Items, But Not All

A few known items for these babies are listed.

Fancy Pants Baby Sunny Bunch: White sipper cup(teddy bear in pink), pink net bow, dish & spoon color?
Peek-a-boo Baby Noddins: white butterfly bib/purple trim
Peek-a-boo Baby Graffiti: white butterfly bib/blue trim
Playtime Baby Brother Paws: Lt. blue/dark pink xylophone with orange stick, dish and spoon color?

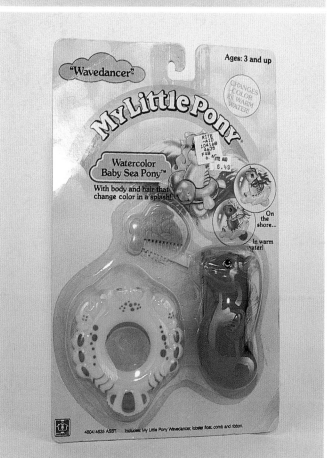

Watercolor Baby Sea Baby Wavedancer: Yellow and purple lobster float, lime green fish comb, yellow ribbon M=$15, GR=$12, G=$10, P=$5

Index Of Pony Names